Chapter 1: Understanding Networking

In today's interconnected world, networking is not just a buzzword; it is a crucial skill that can significantly influence both personal and professional success. At its core, networking is about establishing and nurturing relationships that can lead to mutually beneficial opportunities. Whether you are looking for a job, seeking new clients, or aiming to grow your knowledge, the strength of your network often plays a pivotal role in achieving your goals.

Definition and Significance of Networking

Networking can be defined as the process of creating and maintaining relationships with individuals who can provide support, resources, and opportunities. These relationships can be formal or informal, encompassing a wide range of interactions—from casual conversations at social gatherings to strategic partnerships in professional settings.

The significance of networking cannot be overstated. Research shows that a vast majority of job opportunities and business deals are filled through personal connections rather than traditional job postings or advertisements. Networking can open doors to hidden opportunities, provide access to valuable information, and create avenues for collaboration that may not otherwise exist.

In essence, effective networking is about leveraging relationships to achieve personal and professional objectives. It is an ongoing process that requires commitment, authenticity, and strategic thinking.

Different Types of Networks

Understanding the various types of networks is essential for effective networking. Each type serves a unique purpose and offers different benefits. Here are the primary categories:

1. Personal Networks

These are the connections you cultivate in your everyday life, including family, friends, and acquaintances. Personal networks provide emotional support, advice, and introductions to new contacts. They often serve as a foundational layer for both social and professional networking.

2. Professional Networks

Professional networks consist of individuals you meet through your career. This includes colleagues, industry peers, and mentors. Engaging with a professional network can lead to job opportunities, collaborations, and access to industry knowledge. Attending conferences, joining professional associations, and participating in industry-specific events are excellent ways to grow this network.

3. Social Networks

Social networks typically refer to platforms and communities where individuals connect based on shared interests or experiences. This includes online platforms like LinkedIn, Facebook, and Twitter, as well as local community groups. Social networking can enhance your visibility and broaden your reach, making it easier to connect with a diverse range of individuals.

4. Strategic Networks

Strategic networks are purposefully developed connections that align with specific career or business objectives. These networks often consist of individuals who can provide mentorship, advice, or partnerships. Identifying and nurturing strategic relationships can significantly enhance your ability to achieve your goals.

The Interplay Between Networking and Net Worth

Understanding networking is not just about making connections; it's about strategically building relationships that contribute to your overall net worth. Your net worth, defined as the difference between your assets and liabilities, is often influenced by the opportunities and resources your network can provide. Whether it's landing a high-paying job, securing a business deal, or gaining insights into investment opportunities, a robust network can substantially impact your financial success.

As we delve deeper into the chapters that follow, we will explore the psychology of networking, how to set effective networking goals, and strategies for building your personal brand—all of which will empower you to master the art of networking and enhance your net worth.

By understanding the fundamentals of networking and recognizing the types of networks available to you, you lay the groundwork for a more prosperous future, both in your career and your financial endeavors. In the next chapter, we will explore the psychology behind effective networking, focusing on how to build trust and rapport, as well as overcoming common networking anxieties.

Chapter 2: The Psychology of Networking

Networking is not merely a transactional endeavor; it is deeply rooted in psychology. Understanding the mental and emotional aspects of networking can enhance your ability to connect with others and cultivate meaningful relationships. This chapter will explore the essential elements of building trust and rapport and provide strategies to overcome common networking anxieties.

Building Trust and Rapport

At the heart of effective networking is trust. Building trust requires time, consistency, and genuine interaction. Here are key strategies to foster trust and rapport in your networking efforts:

1. Authenticity

Being authentic means presenting your true self. People are drawn to genuineness and can often sense insincerity. When you engage with others, be open about your intentions, values, and interests. This openness encourages reciprocal honesty, laying the groundwork for a trusting relationship.

2. Active Listening

Listening is a crucial component of effective communication. When you listen actively, you show that you value the other person's thoughts and feelings. This involves not just hearing their words but also paying attention to non-verbal cues and asking follow-up questions. By demonstrating genuine interest, you create a deeper connection and foster trust.

3. Shared Interests

Finding common ground is an excellent way to build rapport. Look for shared interests or experiences that can serve as conversation starters. This not only makes interactions more enjoyable but also creates a sense of belonging and understanding, reinforcing the bond between you and your networking partner.

4. Reliability

Consistency in your actions builds trust over time. If you say you will do something, follow through. Being reliable means others can count on you, which enhances your credibility and strengthens relationships. Whether it's responding promptly to messages or attending scheduled meetings, reliability is key to establishing long-lasting connections.

5. Respect and Empathy

Respecting others' perspectives and showing empathy towards their experiences fosters a positive networking environment. Understanding and valuing diverse viewpoints not only enhances your relationships but also encourages a culture of support and collaboration.

Overcoming Networking Anxiety

Despite the benefits of networking, many people experience anxiety at the thought of reaching out to new contacts. Understanding this anxiety and developing strategies to manage it can empower you to engage more effectively. Here are several techniques to help you overcome networking anxiety:

1. Preparation

Preparation can alleviate anxiety significantly. Before attending an event or meeting, familiarize yourself with the participants, their backgrounds, and any topics of discussion. Having a few conversation starters or questions ready can boost your confidence and ease the pressure of spontaneity.

2. Mindfulness Techniques

Mindfulness practices, such as deep breathing or visualization, can help calm nerves before networking events. Take a moment to focus on your breath, clear your mind, and visualize a positive outcome. This mental preparation can shift your mindset from anxiety to confidence.

3. Set Realistic Goals

Instead of overwhelming yourself with the idea of making numerous connections, set achievable networking goals for each event. For instance, aim to have meaningful conversations with three people instead of trying to meet everyone. This approach makes networking feel more manageable and allows for deeper connections.

4. Shift Your Focus

Instead of concentrating on how others perceive you, shift your focus to the value you can provide. Networking is a two-way street, and by thinking about how you can help others, you take the pressure off yourself and foster a more collaborative atmosphere.

5. Practice Regularly

Like any skill, networking becomes easier with practice. Engage in low-pressure environments, such as informal gatherings or small meetups, to build your confidence. The more you expose yourself to networking situations, the more comfortable you will become over time.

Conclusion

Understanding the psychology of networking is essential for building strong, lasting connections. By focusing on trust, authenticity, and effective communication, you can create meaningful relationships that benefit both your personal and professional life. Additionally, by addressing and managing networking anxiety, you empower yourself to engage more confidently and effectively.

As we move to the next chapter, we will explore how to identify your networking goals, assess your aspirations, and set measurable objectives that align with your journey toward mastering networking and increasing your net worth.

Chapter 3: Identifying Your Networking Goals

Networking is not merely a social activity; it's a strategic approach to advancing your personal and professional aspirations. To harness the true power of networking, it's essential to start with clear and well-defined goals. In this chapter, we will explore how to assess your aspirations and set measurable networking objectives that align with your overall vision.

Assessing Personal and Professional Aspirations

Before diving into networking strategies, take the time to reflect on your personal and professional goals. Here are some steps to help you assess your aspirations:

1. Self-Reflection

Begin by asking yourself critical questions:

- What are my short-term and long-term career goals?
- What personal values do I prioritize in my life and work?
- What skills do I want to develop or enhance?

Write down your thoughts. This self-assessment will serve as a foundation for understanding the type of connections you need to pursue.

2. Vision Mapping

Create a vision map that visually represents your aspirations. Use mind mapping techniques to identify how different areas of your life—career, personal growth, relationships—interconnect. This map will help you visualize your goals and identify the networking opportunities that will be most beneficial.

3. Feedback from Others

Sometimes, we are too close to our goals to see them clearly. Seeking feedback from trusted colleagues, mentors, or friends can provide valuable insights into your strengths and areas for improvement. Ask them:

- What do you think are my greatest strengths?
- In what areas do you believe I could grow?
- Who do you think I should connect with to achieve my goals?

Setting Measurable Networking Objectives

Once you have a clearer understanding of your aspirations, the next step is to translate them into specific, measurable networking objectives. Consider using the SMART criteria (Specific, Measurable, Achievable, Relevant, Time-bound) to guide your goal-setting process.

1. Specific

Be precise about what you want to achieve through networking. Instead of saying, "I want to expand my network," specify, "I want to connect with five industry leaders in my field."

2. Measurable

Define how you will measure your progress. This could include:

- The number of new contacts made each month.
- Attending a specific number of networking events or conferences.
- Engaging in conversations with a certain number of people in your network each week.

3. Achievable

Ensure your objectives are realistic. Setting overly ambitious goals can lead to frustration. Assess your current resources, including time, energy, and existing connections, to determine what is achievable.

4. Relevant

Align your networking goals with your overall career and personal development objectives. Each connection you pursue should serve a purpose that supports your larger aspirations.

5. Time-bound

Set deadlines for your goals. For example, "I will attend three networking events within the next three months" gives you a clear timeframe for accountability.

Example Networking Goals

Here are some examples of networking goals that follow the SMART framework:

Goal 1: Build Industry Connections

- **Specific**: Connect with 10 professionals in the technology sector.
- **Measurable**: Track new connections on LinkedIn.
- **Achievable**: Use industry events and online platforms to reach out.
- **Relevant**: Aligns with my career goal of transitioning to a tech-focused role.
- **Time-bound**: Complete within the next two months.

Goal 2: Develop Mentorship Relationships

- **Specific**: Find a mentor in my field who can guide my career.
- **Measurable**: Have at least two mentorship sessions per month.
- **Achievable**: Reach out to former colleagues and professionals at networking events.
- **Relevant**: Supports my personal development and career growth.
- **Time-bound**: Establish a mentorship relationship within six months.

Goal 3: Enhance Public Speaking Skills

- **Specific**: Join a local Toastmasters club to improve public speaking.
- **Measurable**: Participate in at least one meeting per month.
- **Achievable**: Identify local clubs and schedule meetings.
- **Relevant**: Enhances my networking ability and personal brand.
- **Time-bound**: Achieve this within three months.

Conclusion

Identifying your networking goals is a crucial step in maximizing your networking efforts. By assessing your personal and professional aspirations and setting SMART objectives, you will create a roadmap that guides your networking activities. This intentional approach not only helps you connect with the right individuals but also ensures that your networking efforts contribute meaningfully to your overall growth and success. In the next chapter, we will explore how to build your personal brand, a vital aspect of making lasting connections in your network.

4o mini

You said:

Chapter 4: Building Your Personal Brand

In today's interconnected world, your personal brand is more than just a buzzword—it's the foundation upon which meaningful professional relationships are built. Your personal brand is the unique combination of skills, experiences, and personality that you present to the world. It's how people perceive you, remember you, and ultimately, how they decide whether to connect, collaborate, or do business with you. This chapter will guide you through the essential elements of building a compelling personal brand that resonates with your networking goals and amplifies your net worth.

Understanding Personal Branding

Personal branding is the intentional effort to shape the public perception of yourself by positioning your expertise, values, and personality in a way that differentiates you from others. Unlike traditional branding, which focuses on products or companies, personal branding is about YOU—your story, your journey, and what makes you uniquely valuable.

A strong personal brand accomplishes several things:

- **Establishes credibility**: It positions you as an authority in your field.
- **Builds trust**: Consistency in your message and actions fosters reliability.
- **Creates opportunities**: A recognizable brand attracts partnerships, clients, and career advancements.
- **Amplifies your network**: People are more likely to connect with and refer individuals who have a clear, compelling brand.

Crafting Your Personal Story

Every memorable brand begins with a story. Your personal story is the narrative thread that weaves together your experiences, values, challenges, and triumphs. It's what makes you relatable and memorable in a sea of professionals.

The Elements of a Compelling Personal Story

1. **Authenticity**: Your story must be true to who you are. Authenticity resonates with people because it's genuine and relatable. Don't try to mimic someone else's journey—embrace your own.

2. **Clarity**: A good story is clear and easy to understand. Avoid jargon or overly complex narratives. Distill your journey into key moments that define who you are.

3. **Relevance**: Tailor your story to your audience. While the core of your narrative remains consistent, emphasize different aspects depending on who you're speaking to—whether it's a potential employer, client, or collaborator.

4. **Emotion**: Stories that evoke emotion are the ones that stick. Share the challenges you've overcome, the lessons you've learned, and the passions that drive you.

5. **Purpose**: What's the "why" behind your journey? A clear sense of purpose gives your story direction and inspires others to connect with your mission.

Steps to Crafting Your Personal Story

- **Reflect on your journey**: Take time to consider the pivotal moments in your life and career. What experiences shaped you? What challenges did you overcome? What accomplishments are you most proud of?

- **Identify your values**: What principles guide your decisions and actions? Your values are the backbone of your brand.

- **Define your unique value proposition (UVP)**: What do you offer that others don't? Your UVP is the intersection of your skills, passions, and the needs of your audience.

- **Write it down**: Draft your personal story in multiple formats—a short elevator pitch (30 seconds), a medium-length introduction (2 minutes), and a longer narrative for written bios or interviews.

- **Practice and refine**: Share your story with trusted friends or mentors and refine it based on their feedback. The more you tell it, the more natural it will become.

The Importance of Online Presence

In the digital age, your online presence is often the first impression people have of you. Before a handshake or a meeting, potential connections are likely to Google your name, check your LinkedIn profile, or scroll through your social media. A strong, intentional online presence is no longer optional—it's essential.

LinkedIn: The Professional Networking Powerhouse

LinkedIn is the cornerstone of professional online networking. With over 900 million users worldwide, it's the platform where professionals connect, share insights, and discover opportunities. Here's how to optimize your LinkedIn profile to build a powerful personal brand:

1. **Professional Headshot**: Your profile picture is the first visual element people see. Invest in a high-quality, professional headshot that reflects your personality and industry.

2. **Compelling Headline**: Go beyond your job title. Use the headline space to showcase your expertise, value proposition, or passion. For example, instead of "Marketing Manager," try "Marketing Strategist | Helping Brands Tell Authentic Stories."

3. **Engaging Summary**: Your summary is where your personal story comes to life. Write in the first person, highlight your achievements, and convey your passion. Use keywords relevant to your industry to improve searchability.

4. **Detailed Experience**: List your work experience with specific accomplishments, not just job duties. Use metrics and results to demonstrate impact.

5. **Skills and Endorsements**: Add relevant skills to your profile and seek endorsements from colleagues. Recommendations from peers and supervisors add credibility.

6. **Content Sharing**: Regularly share articles, insights, and updates related to your field. Engage with others' content through thoughtful comments and likes. Consistent activity keeps you visible in your network.

7. **Networking**: Connect with colleagues, industry leaders, and others in your field. Personalize your connection requests with a brief note explaining why you'd like to connect.

Beyond LinkedIn: Leveraging Other Social Media Platforms

While LinkedIn is the gold standard for professional networking, other platforms can complement your personal brand depending on your industry and goals:

- **Twitter/X**: Great for sharing quick insights, engaging in industry conversations, and building thought leadership.

- **Instagram**: Ideal for visual industries like design, fashion, or lifestyle. Use it to showcase your work, behind-the-scenes moments, and personal interests.

- **YouTube**: A powerful platform for those who want to share expertise through video content, tutorials, or interviews.

- **Personal Website/Blog**: Having your own website gives you complete control over your brand narrative. It's a central hub where people can learn about you, view your portfolio, and contact you.

- **TikTok**: Increasingly popular for personal branding, especially among younger audiences. Short, engaging videos can showcase your personality and expertise.

Best Practices for Online Presence

- **Consistency**: Ensure your profile picture, bio, and messaging are consistent across all platforms. This creates a cohesive brand image.

- **Authenticity**: Be yourself online. People connect with real, genuine individuals—not overly curated personas.

- **Engagement**: Networking is a two-way street. Engage with others' content, respond to comments, and participate in conversations.

- **Value-Driven Content**: Share content that provides value to your audience—whether it's insights, advice, or inspiration.

- **Privacy and Professionalism**: Be mindful of what you post. Even personal accounts can be viewed by potential employers or clients. Maintain a level of professionalism across all platforms.

Bringing It All Together

Building your personal brand is an ongoing journey, not a one-time project. It requires reflection, intentionality, and consistent effort. By crafting a compelling personal story and cultivating a strong online presence, you position yourself as a memorable, trustworthy, and valuable connection in any network.

As you move forward, remember that your personal brand is a living, evolving entity. It will grow and change as you do. Embrace the process, stay true to yourself, and let your unique brand be the magnet that attracts the right opportunities, relationships, and successes into your life.

In the next chapter, we'll explore where to take your newly crafted personal brand—identifying the key networking opportunities that will help you expand your network and elevate your net worth.

Part 4: Understanding Net Worth Chapter 13: Defining Net Worth Assets vs. liabilities: what counts? The importance of tracking your net worth. Chapter 14: Financial Literacy Fundamentals Basic financial concepts everyone should know.

Resources for improving financial literacy. Chapter 15: Creating a Budget and Savings Plan Steps to develop a personal budget. Strategies for saving effectively. Chapter 16: Investing Basics Overview of investment options (stocks, bonds, real estate). Risk assessment and portfolio diversification. Part 5: Increasing Your Net Worth Chapter 17: Income Streams Identifying and creating multiple income sources. Passive income strategies. Chapter 18: Leveraging Networking for Financial Gains How to turn connections into clients or business opportunities. Networking tactics for entrepreneurs. Chapter 19: Building a Personal Development Plan Setting goals for career advancement. Investing in skills and education. Chapter 20: Risk Management and Insurance Importance of protecting your assets. Types of insurance to consider. Part 6: Sustaining Success Chapter 21: Giving Back and Community Engagement The role of philanthropy in networking and net worth. Building a legacy through community involvement. Chapter 22: Adapting to Change Staying relevant in a changing economy. Networking in a digital age. Chapter 23: Continuous Learning and Growth Emphasizing lifelong learning. Resources for ongoing education. Chapter 24: Measuring Your Success Tools for assessing networking and financial growth. Adjusting strategies based on results.

ChatGPT said:

ChatGPT

Chapter 4: Building Your Personal Brand

In today's interconnected world, building a strong personal brand is essential for successful networking. Your personal brand is the perception others have of you based on your experiences, values, and interactions. It reflects who you are and what you stand for, making it a powerful tool for establishing credibility and attracting opportunities. In this chapter, we'll explore how to craft your personal story and the importance of maintaining a robust online presence.

Crafting Your Personal Story

Your personal story is a narrative that encapsulates your experiences, values, and aspirations. It serves as the foundation of your personal brand and helps others understand your unique perspective. Here are steps to help you craft a compelling personal story:

1. Identify Key Experiences

Reflect on significant experiences that have shaped your life and career. Consider:

- Major achievements or milestones
- Challenges you've overcome
- Lessons learned along the way

These experiences will form the backbone of your personal story.

2. Define Your Values and Passions

Your values and passions should be integral to your personal brand. Identify what drives you:

- What principles guide your decisions?
- What topics or causes are you passionate about?

Incorporating your values and passions into your story creates authenticity and resonates with others.

3. Establish Your Unique Selling Proposition (USP)

What sets you apart from others in your field? Your USP is what makes you memorable and valuable. It could be a combination of your skills, experiences, and personality traits. Articulate this clearly in your narrative to create a lasting impression.

4. Craft a Narrative

Combine the elements you've identified into a cohesive narrative. Your story should have a clear structure:

- **Introduction**: Briefly introduce yourself and your background.
- **Body**: Share key experiences, values, and your USP.
- **Conclusion**: End with your vision for the future and what you hope to achieve.

Practice delivering your story in a concise manner, as you may need to share it in various networking contexts, such as at events or in interviews.

5. Be Authentic

Authenticity is crucial in building trust. Share your story in a way that feels genuine and reflects your true self. Avoid embellishing facts or adopting a persona that doesn't align with who you are. People are drawn to authenticity, which fosters deeper connections.

Importance of Online Presence

In today's digital age, your online presence significantly impacts your personal brand. It's essential to curate a professional and positive online image that reflects your personal story and values. Here's how to enhance your online presence:

1. Optimize Your LinkedIn Profile

LinkedIn is a powerful platform for professionals. Make sure your profile is complete and showcases your personal brand:

- **Profile Picture**: Use a high-quality, professional photo.
- **Headline**: Write a compelling headline that captures your role and value proposition.
- **Summary**: Craft a summary that includes your personal story, experiences, and aspirations.
- **Experience and Skills**: List your relevant experiences and highlight key skills.

2. Engage with Content

Share and engage with relevant content on LinkedIn and other social media platforms. This not only positions you as a thought leader but also helps expand your network. Consider:

- Posting articles or insights related to your field.
- Commenting on posts to share your perspectives.
- Joining groups to connect with like-minded professionals.

3. Utilize Other Social Media Platforms

While LinkedIn is crucial for professional networking, other platforms can also enhance your personal brand. Depending on your industry, consider using:

- **Twitter**: Share industry news and insights, and engage in conversations.
- **Instagram**: Showcase your work, projects, or personal interests.
- **Personal Website or Blog**: Create a platform to share your expertise, portfolio, and personal story in-depth.

4. Consistency Across Platforms

Ensure your branding is consistent across all platforms. Use similar language, imagery, and messaging that aligns with your personal story. This consistency builds recognition and reinforces your brand identity.

5. Monitor Your Online Reputation

Regularly check your online presence to manage your reputation. Google yourself to see what others find when they search for you. Address any discrepancies or negative content proactively to maintain a positive image.

Conclusion

Building a personal brand is a vital step in mastering networking and enhancing your net worth. By crafting a compelling personal story and establishing a strong online presence, you create a foundation that fosters meaningful connections and opens doors to new opportunities. In the next chapter, we will explore where to network effectively, identifying key opportunities to expand your network and achieve your goals.

4o mini

You said:

Chapter 5: Where to Network

Networking is a vital skill in today's interconnected world, and knowing where to network can significantly enhance your opportunities for personal and professional growth. This chapter explores key networking opportunities, including conferences, seminars, and online platforms, as well as the importance of leveraging community events and local groups.

Identifying Key Networking Opportunities

Conferences

Conferences are among the most effective venues for networking. They bring together professionals from various industries, providing a unique opportunity to connect with like-minded individuals, industry leaders, and potential collaborators. Here are some tips for making the most of conferences:

- **Research the Event**: Before attending, familiarize yourself with the agenda, speakers, and attendees. Identify key sessions that align with your interests and goals. This preparation will help you engage in meaningful conversations.

- **Set Networking Goals**: Determine what you want to achieve at the conference. Whether it's meeting a specific number of new contacts, finding a mentor, or learning about industry trends, having clear goals will guide your interactions.

- **Engage Actively**: Participate in discussions, ask questions during sessions, and attend networking events. Don't hesitate to introduce yourself to speakers and fellow attendees. Remember, everyone is there to connect.

- **Follow Up**: After the conference, reach out to the contacts you made. A simple email or LinkedIn message referencing your conversation can solidify the connection and open doors for future interactions.

Seminars and Workshops

Seminars and workshops offer a more intimate setting for networking. These events often focus on specific topics, allowing participants to delve deeper into subjects of interest. Here's how to leverage these opportunities:

- **Choose Relevant Topics**: Select seminars that align with your professional interests or areas where you want to grow. This ensures that you meet individuals who share your passions.

- **Participate in Discussions**: Engage with the speakers and fellow attendees. Sharing your insights and experiences can lead to valuable connections and discussions.

- **Utilize Breakout Sessions**: Many seminars include breakout sessions or group activities. Use these opportunities to collaborate with others and build rapport.

- **Network During Breaks**: Don't underestimate the power of informal conversations during breaks. Approach others, introduce yourself, and discuss the seminar's content.

Online Platforms

In the digital age, online platforms have become essential for networking. They provide access to a global audience and allow for connections that transcend geographical boundaries. Here are some effective online networking strategies:

- **LinkedIn**: As the leading professional networking site, LinkedIn is a powerful tool for building your network. Optimize your profile, engage with content, and connect with professionals in your field. Join relevant groups to participate in discussions and expand your reach.

- **Industry-Specific Forums**: Many industries have dedicated forums and online communities. Participate in these platforms to share knowledge, ask questions, and connect with others who share your interests.

- **Social Media**: Platforms like Twitter, Facebook, and Instagram can also be valuable for networking. Follow industry leaders, engage with their content, and participate in relevant conversations to build your online presence.

- **Webinars and Virtual Events**: With the rise of remote work, webinars and virtual conferences have become popular. Attend these events to learn from experts and connect with participants through chat features and breakout rooms.

Leveraging Community Events and Local Groups

While large conferences and online platforms are important, local community events and groups can provide equally valuable networking opportunities. Here's how to make the most of them:

Community Events

Community events, such as local festivals, charity events, and business expos, offer a chance to meet people in your area. Here are some tips for leveraging these events:

- **Get Involved**: Volunteer for local events or participate in community service. This not only helps you meet new people but also demonstrates your commitment to the community.

- **Attend Local Meetups**: Websites like Meetup.com offer a variety of local gatherings based on interests and professions. Attend these meetups to connect with individuals in your field or explore new interests.

- **Engage with Local Businesses**: Support local businesses by attending their events or promotions. Building relationships with local entrepreneurs can lead to valuable connections and collaborations.

Local Groups and Associations

Joining local professional groups and associations can provide a structured way to network. Consider the following:

- **Professional Associations**: Many industries have local chapters of professional associations. Joining these groups can provide access to networking events, workshops, and resources tailored to your field.

- **Chambers of Commerce**: Local chambers of commerce often host networking events, business expos, and workshops. Becoming a member can open doors to a wide range of local businesses and professionals.

- **Networking Groups**: Look for networking groups specifically designed for professionals in your area. These groups often meet regularly and provide a supportive environment for building connections.

- **Alumni Associations**: If you attended college or university, consider joining your alumni association. These organizations often host events and provide networking opportunities with fellow alumni.

Conclusion

Identifying where to network is crucial for expanding your connections and achieving your personal and professional goals. By leveraging conferences, seminars, online platforms, community events, and local groups, you can create a robust network that supports your aspirations. Remember, networking is not just about collecting contacts; it's about building meaningful relationships that can lead to mutual growth and success. As you explore these opportunities, keep an open mind, be genuine in your interactions, and always be willing to give as much as you receive. Your network is a powerful asset, and nurturing it will pay dividends throughout your career.

Part 4: Understanding Net Worth Chapter 13: Defining Net Worth Assets vs. liabilities: what counts? The importance of tracking your net worth. Chapter 14: Financial Literacy Fundamentals Basic financial concepts everyone should know.

Resources for improving financial literacy. Chapter 15: Creating a Budget and Savings Plan Steps to develop a personal budget. Strategies for saving effectively. Chapter 16: Investing Basics Overview of investment options (stocks, bonds, real estate). Risk assessment and portfolio diversification. Part 5: Increasing Your Net Worth Chapter 17: Income Streams Identifying and creating multiple income sources. Passive income strategies. Chapter 18: Leveraging Networking for Financial Gains How to turn connections into clients or business opportunities. Networking tactics for entrepreneurs. Chapter 19: Building a Personal Development Plan Setting goals for career advancement. Investing in skills and education. Chapter 20: Risk Management and Insurance Importance of protecting your assets. Types of insurance to consider. Part 6: Sustaining Success Chapter 21: Giving Back and Community Engagement The role of philanthropy in networking and net worth. Building a legacy through community involvement. Chapter 22: Adapting to Change Staying relevant in a changing economy. Networking in a digital age. Chapter 23: Continuous Learning and Growth Emphasizing lifelong learning. Resources for ongoing education. Chapter 24: Measuring Your Success Tools for assessing networking and financial growth. Adjusting strategies based on results.

ChatGPT said:

ChatGPT

Chapter 5: Where to Network

Networking is not just about who you know; it's also about where you connect with others. Identifying key networking opportunities is crucial to expanding your network effectively. This chapter will explore various avenues for networking, from formal conferences and seminars to informal community events and online platforms. By understanding where to network, you can strategically position yourself to meet the right people who can help you achieve your goals.

Identifying Key Networking Opportunities

1. Conferences and Seminars

Conferences and seminars are excellent environments for professional networking. These events often attract like-minded individuals, industry leaders, and influencers, making them ideal for building meaningful connections.

Benefits:

- **Access to Industry Experts**: Learn from keynote speakers and panel discussions, gaining insights into trends and best practices.
- **Opportunities for Engagement**: Participate in Q&A sessions, workshops, or networking breaks to meet fellow attendees.

Tips for Success:

- **Prepare in Advance**: Research the speakers and attendees before the event. Prepare thoughtful questions or comments to engage in conversations.
- **Bring Business Cards**: Always have business cards on hand to facilitate exchanging contact information.

2. Networking Events and Meetups

Networking events, often organized by professional associations or local groups, are designed specifically for making connections. Meetup platforms can help you find gatherings that align with your interests.

Benefits:

- **Targeted Connections**: These events often focus on specific industries or interests, allowing you to connect with individuals who share similar goals.
- **Informal Atmosphere**: Networking events typically offer a more relaxed setting, making it easier to start conversations.

Tips for Success:

- **Follow Up**: After meeting new contacts, send a brief email or message thanking them for their time and expressing interest in staying connected.
- **Engage Actively**: Don't be afraid to introduce yourself to new people and initiate conversations with those who seem approachable.

3. Online Networking Platforms

The rise of digital networking has transformed how we connect with others. Platforms like LinkedIn, Twitter, and professional forums provide vast opportunities to network without geographical constraints.

Benefits:

- **Wider Reach**: Online platforms allow you to connect with professionals from around the world, expanding your network beyond local limitations.
- **24/7 Accessibility**: You can engage with content and connect with others at any time, making it convenient to integrate networking into your schedule.

Tips for Success:

- **Optimize Your Profile**: Ensure your online profiles are complete and reflect your personal brand. Use professional photos and clear descriptions of your skills and experiences.
- **Engage with Content**: Regularly share and comment on relevant industry content. This not only positions you as an engaged professional but also attracts connections interested in similar topics.

4. Community Events and Local Groups

Community events—such as workshops, volunteering opportunities, or local business gatherings—offer great networking opportunities that may be overlooked.

Benefits:

- **Building Local Connections**: Engaging with your community can lead to valuable relationships with local professionals, which can be particularly beneficial for small businesses or entrepreneurs.
- **Diverse Networking**: Community events often attract a wide range of individuals, allowing you to connect with people from various backgrounds and industries.

Tips for Success:

- **Volunteer**: Consider volunteering at local events or organizations. This not only demonstrates your commitment to the community but also increases your visibility among local leaders.
- **Participate in Local Business Groups**: Join local chambers of commerce or business associations to meet other entrepreneurs and professionals in your area.

5. Professional Associations and Organizations

Joining professional associations related to your field can provide ongoing networking opportunities through workshops, conferences, and member-exclusive events.

Benefits:

- **Credibility and Recognition**: Membership in reputable organizations enhances your credibility and connects you with industry leaders.
- **Access to Resources**: Many associations offer educational resources, training sessions, and networking events to help members develop their skills.

Tips for Success:
- **Attend Regularly**: Make it a habit to participate in events hosted by these organizations. Consistency will help you build deeper connections over time.
- **Take on a Leadership Role**: Consider volunteering for committees or leadership positions within the association. This can enhance your visibility and credibility.

Leveraging Community Events and Local Groups

Local networking can be just as powerful as connections made in larger settings. Here's how to leverage community events and local groups effectively:

1. Know Your Local Scene

Familiarize yourself with local events, industry meetups, and community activities. Platforms like Meetup, Eventbrite, and local Facebook groups can help you find relevant gatherings.

2. Create Your Own Events

If you can't find the networking opportunities you're looking for, consider creating your own. Organize a small meetup, discussion group, or workshop focused on topics of interest. This positions you as a thought leader and creates networking opportunities for others, fostering mutual benefit.

3. Build Relationships

Networking is about quality, not quantity. Focus on building genuine relationships rather than simply collecting business cards. Follow up with individuals you meet and make an effort to stay in touch. Over time, these relationships can lead to collaborative opportunities and referrals.

Conclusion

Identifying where to network is crucial to building a robust professional network. By exploring a variety of venues—from conferences and seminars to community events and online platforms—you can strategically position yourself to connect with individuals who align with your aspirations. As you expand your network, remember to engage authentically and cultivate lasting relationships. In the next chapter, we will delve into the art of conversation, focusing on effective communication skills to help you engage meaningfully with your new connections.

Chapter 6: The Art of Conversation

Conversation is the lifeblood of networking. While attending events, joining groups, and connecting online provide the opportunities, it is the quality of your conversations that determines whether those opportunities transform into meaningful relationships. Mastering the art of conversation is not about being the loudest voice in the room or having a rehearsed pitch ready at all times—it is about engaging authentically, listening deeply, and communicating in a way that leaves a lasting impression.

In this chapter, we will explore effective communication skills and active listening techniques that will help you become a more confident, engaging, and memorable conversationalist.

Effective Communication Skills

Effective communication is the foundation of successful networking. It is the ability to convey your thoughts clearly, connect with others emotionally, and create a two-way exchange that benefits both parties. Here are the key elements of effective communication in networking:

1. Clarity and Conciseness

In a world of short attention spans, being clear and concise is more important than ever. When introducing yourself or discussing your work, avoid jargon, rambling explanations, or overly technical language. Instead, aim to communicate your message in a way that is easy to understand and memorable.

Tip: Practice your "elevator pitch"—a 30-second summary of who you are, what you do, and what makes you unique. Keep it natural, not robotic.

2. Body Language

Your non-verbal cues often speak louder than your words. Maintain open body language—uncrossed arms, a relaxed posture, and a genuine smile. Make eye contact to convey confidence and interest, but avoid staring, which can feel intimidating.

Tip: Mirror the body language of the person you are speaking with subtly. This technique builds rapport and creates a sense of connection.

3. Tone and Pace

The way you say something can be just as important as what you say. Speak at a moderate pace, with a tone that reflects warmth and enthusiasm. Avoid speaking too quickly, which can make you seem nervous, or too slowly, which can come across as disengaged.

4. Asking Open-Ended Questions

Great conversationalists know how to keep the dialogue flowing by asking open-ended questions. These are questions that cannot be answered with a simple "yes" or "no" and invite the other person to share more about themselves.

Examples:
- "What inspired you to pursue your current career?"
- "What are some of the biggest challenges you are facing in your industry right now?"
- "How did you get started in this field?"

5. Authenticity

Authenticity is magnetic. People can sense when you are being genuine versus when you are putting on a façade. Be yourself, share your true thoughts and experiences, and let your personality shine through. Authenticity fosters trust and makes your interactions more memorable.

Active Listening and Engagement Techniques

While speaking well is important, listening is arguably the more critical skill in networking. Active listening demonstrates respect, builds trust, and allows you to gather valuable information that can deepen the conversation. Here's how to become a better active listener:

1. Be Fully Present

In today's digital age, distractions are everywhere. When engaging in a conversation, put away your phone, silence notifications, and focus entirely on the person in front of you. Being fully present signals that you value the interaction.

2. Show That You Are Listening

Use verbal and non-verbal cues to show you are engaged. Nod occasionally, maintain eye contact, and use affirming phrases like "I see," "That's interesting," or "Tell me more about that." These small gestures encourage the other person to continue sharing.

3. Avoid Interrupting

Resist the urge to interrupt or finish someone else's sentences. Let the other person speak fully before responding. Interrupting can come across as dismissive, while patience demonstrates respect.

4. Paraphrase and Clarify

To show that you truly understand what the other person is saying, paraphrase their points or ask clarifying questions. For example:
- "So, if I understand correctly, you're saying that..."
- "Can you explain more about what you mean by...?"

This technique not only reinforces your engagement but also ensures that you accurately interpret their message.

5. Empathize

Empathy is the ability to understand and share the feelings of another person. When someone shares a challenge or success, acknowledge their emotions. For example:
- "That must have been a difficult experience."
- "It sounds like you worked really hard to achieve that—congratulations!"

Empathy strengthens emotional connections and makes you a more relatable conversationalist.

6. Remember Key Details

Pay attention to the specifics of what someone shares—names, interests, goals, or challenges. Remembering these details and referencing them in future conversations shows that you genuinely care and have been paying attention.

Overcoming Common Conversation Challenges

Even the best conversationalists face challenges. Here are some strategies to handle common networking hurdles:

1. Starting a Conversation

Approaching someone new can be intimidating. Start with a simple icebreaker, such as a compliment, a question about the event, or an observation about your surroundings. For example:
- "This event has been fantastic so far. What's been your favorite part?"
- "I love your presentation earlier—what inspired your topic?"

2. Keeping the Conversation Flowing

If the conversation hits a lull, use open-ended questions or shift to a new topic of mutual interest. Avoid controversial subjects like politics or religion, and focus on areas like career, hobbies, or travel.

3. Exiting a Conversation Gracefully

Not every conversation needs to last forever. When it's time to move on, do so politely. For example:
- "It was so great chatting with you. I'd love to connect further—can we exchange contact information?"
- "I don't want to monopolize your time, but I've really enjoyed our conversation. Let's stay in touch."

Practical Exercises to Improve Your Conversation Skills

1. **Practice Active Listening:** In your next conversation, focus entirely on the other person. Avoid planning your response while they are speaking, and instead, concentrate on understanding their words.

2. **Role-Play Scenarios:** Practice networking conversations with a friend or mentor. Role-playing can help you refine your elevator pitch, body language, and questioning techniques.

3. **Reflect on Past Conversations:** After a networking event, review your interactions. What went well? What could you improve? Use these insights to grow.

4. **Read and Watch Experts:** Study books, TED Talks, or interviews featuring skilled communicators. Pay attention to how they engage, listen, and respond.

Conclusion

The art of conversation is a skill that can be developed with practice and intentionality. By mastering effective communication and active listening, you can create deeper, more meaningful connections that enhance your personal and professional network. Remember, networking is not about talking at people—it's about engaging with them in a way that leaves a lasting impact.

In the next chapter, we will explore the importance of follow-up strategies to ensure that the connections you make through great conversations turn into long-lasting relationships.

Part 4: Understanding Net Worth Chapter 13: Defining Net Worth Assets vs. liabilities: what counts? The importance of tracking your net worth. Chapter 14: Financial Literacy Fundamentals Basic financial concepts everyone should know.

Resources for improving financial literacy. Chapter 15: Creating a Budget and Savings Plan Steps to develop a personal budget. Strategies for saving effectively. Chapter 16: Investing Basics Overview of investment options (stocks, bonds, real estate). Risk assessment and portfolio diversification. Part 5: Increasing Your Net Worth Chapter 17: Income Streams Identifying and creating multiple income sources. Passive income strategies. Chapter 18: Leveraging Networking for Financial Gains How to turn connections into clients or business opportunities. Networking tactics for entrepreneurs. Chapter 19: Building a Personal Development Plan Setting goals for career advancement. Investing in skills and education. Chapter 20: Risk Management and Insurance Importance of protecting your assets. Types of insurance to consider. Part 6: Sustaining Success Chapter 21: Giving Back and Community Engagement The role of philanthropy in networking and net worth. Building a legacy through community involvement. Chapter 22: Adapting to Change Staying relevant in a changing economy. Networking in a digital age. Chapter 23: Continuous Learning and Growth Emphasizing lifelong learning. Resources for ongoing education. Chapter 24: Measuring Your Success Tools for assessing networking and financial growth. Adjusting strategies based on results.

ChatGPT said:

ChatGPT

Chapter 6: The Art of Conversation

Networking is not merely about exchanging business cards; it's about creating meaningful connections. At the heart of successful networking lies the art of conversation. Effective communication skills can significantly enhance your networking experiences, allowing you to engage authentically and build lasting relationships. This chapter will explore essential communication techniques and active listening strategies to help you become a more effective conversationalist.

Effective Communication Skills

1. The Importance of Clarity and Conciseness

When conversing, clarity is paramount. Articulating your thoughts clearly helps convey your message effectively, ensuring that the other person understands your perspective. Aim for brevity—avoid rambling or overcomplicating your message.

Tips for Clarity:

- **Organize Your Thoughts**: Before speaking, take a moment to organize your thoughts. Identify key points you want to convey.
- **Use Simple Language**: Avoid jargon unless you're sure the other person is familiar with it. Simplicity fosters better understanding.

2. Nonverbal Communication

Nonverbal cues, such as body language, eye contact, and facial expressions, play a significant role in how your message is received. Being aware of your nonverbal signals can enhance the effectiveness of your conversations.

Key Nonverbal Signals:

- **Eye Contact**: Maintaining appropriate eye contact demonstrates confidence and engagement. It shows you are interested in the conversation.
- **Open Posture**: An open posture (e.g., uncrossed arms, facing the speaker) conveys receptiveness and approachability.
- **Nodding**: Nodding occasionally while the other person speaks signals that you are actively listening and understanding their points.

3. Tailoring Your Approach

Adapt your conversational style to suit your audience. Consider factors such as their background, expertise, and interests. Tailoring your approach shows respect and enhances engagement.

Strategies for Tailoring:

- **Ask Open-Ended Questions**: Encourage others to share their thoughts by asking questions that cannot be answered with a simple "yes" or "no." For example, "What inspired you to pursue this career?"
- **Find Common Ground**: Look for shared interests or experiences to establish rapport. This creates a more engaging and relatable conversation.

Active Listening and Engagement Techniques

1. The Art of Active Listening

Active listening is a critical skill that involves fully concentrating, understanding, and responding to what the other person is saying. It goes beyond merely hearing words; it requires engaging with the speaker on a deeper level.

Techniques for Active Listening:

- **Reflect Back**: Paraphrase what the speaker has said to demonstrate understanding. For instance, "So what you're saying is…"
- **Avoid Interrupting**: Allow the speaker to finish their thoughts before responding. Interrupting can signal disinterest and disrupt the flow of conversation.

2. Encouraging Dialogue

Engagement is a two-way street. Encouraging dialogue ensures that both parties contribute to the conversation, fostering a sense of collaboration.

Tips for Encouragement:

- **Use Follow-Up Questions**: After a speaker shares an idea, ask follow-up questions that invite them to elaborate. For example, "Can you tell me more about that experience?"
- **Share Your Insights**: Once you understand the other person's perspective, share your thoughts or experiences that relate to the discussion. This creates a balanced exchange of ideas.

3. Managing Conversational Flow

Understanding how to manage the flow of conversation can help keep it engaging and productive. Transitioning smoothly between topics and knowing when to steer the conversation can enhance the overall experience.

Strategies for Managing Flow:

- **Identify Natural Pauses**: Use pauses in conversation as opportunities to introduce new topics or pivot discussions. For example, "That's an interesting point; it reminds me of..."
- **Be Mindful of Time**: Respect the other person's time. If they seem distracted or busy, be prepared to wrap up the conversation gracefully.

Overcoming Common Conversational Challenges
1. Dealing with Awkward Silence

Awkward silences can occur during conversations, especially when meeting new people. Instead of panicking, use these moments as opportunities to pivot to another topic or ask a new question.

Tips for Handling Silence:

- **Ask About Their Interests**: If the conversation stalls, asking about hobbies or interests can reignite the dialogue.
- **Share a Relevant Anecdote**: Share a brief story related to the context of the conversation. Personal anecdotes can add depth and warmth to the discussion.

2. Navigating Difficult Topics

Some topics may be sensitive or controversial. Approach these subjects with caution, and be prepared to redirect the conversation if necessary.

Guidelines for Navigating Difficult Topics:

- **Be Respectful**: If the topic becomes uncomfortable, acknowledge it gracefully. For instance, "I understand this is a sensitive subject; let's talk about something else."
- **Focus on Common Interests**: Steer the conversation back to neutral ground by referencing shared interests or experiences.

Conclusion

Mastering the art of conversation is vital for effective networking. By honing your communication skills and practicing active listening, you can create engaging, meaningful interactions that lay the foundation for lasting connections. As you apply these techniques, remember that networking is a journey. In the next chapter, we will explore the importance of follow-up strategies, emphasizing how to stay connected and nurture the relationships you've built.

Chapter 7: Follow-Up Strategies

In the world of networking, the initial meeting is only the beginning. The true value of a connection often emerges in the follow-up. A thoughtful, timely follow-up can transform a brief encounter into a lasting, mutually beneficial relationship. This chapter explores the importance of follow-up in networking and outlines best practices for staying connected with your contacts over time.

The Importance of Timely Follow-Ups

Follow-ups are the bridge between a first impression and an ongoing relationship. Without them, even the most promising connections can fade into obscurity. Here's why timely follow-ups are essential:

1. Reinforcing the Connection

When you meet someone new, their memory of you is fresh but fleeting. A timely follow-up—ideally within 24 to 48 hours—reinforces the connection while the interaction is still top of mind. It demonstrates that you value the relationship and are genuinely interested in maintaining it.

2. Demonstrating Professionalism

Following up promptly signals that you are organized, reliable, and professional. It shows that you take your commitments seriously and respect the other person's time. In a world where many connections are made but few are nurtured, a strong follow-up sets you apart.

3. Building Trust

Trust is the foundation of any meaningful relationship. By following up as promised—whether it's sending a resource you mentioned, introducing a mutual contact, or simply thanking them for their time—you establish yourself as someone who honors their word. Over time, these small acts of reliability build deep trust.

4. Opening Doors to Opportunities

Many opportunities arise not from the initial meeting but from subsequent interactions. A follow-up can lead to collaborations, referrals, job offers, mentorships, or partnerships. Without the follow-up, these possibilities may never come to fruition.

5. Keeping You Top of Mind

People are busy, and even those who genuinely want to help may forget about you if you don't stay visible. Regular, meaningful follow-ups keep you in their awareness, so when an opportunity arises, you're the first person they think of.

Crafting an Effective Follow-Up

Not all follow-ups are created equal. A generic "nice to meet you" message is easily forgotten, while a thoughtful, personalized follow-up leaves a lasting impression. Here are the key elements of an effective follow-up:

1. Personalization

Reference something specific from your conversation. It could be a shared interest, a topic you discussed, or a question they raised. Personalization shows that you were genuinely engaged and that the person is more than just a name in your contact list.

2. Gratitude

Express appreciation for their time, insights, or willingness to connect. A simple "thank you" goes a long way in establishing goodwill.

3. Value

Whenever possible, offer something of value in your follow-up. This might be an article related to a topic you discussed, an introduction to someone in your network, or an insight that might benefit them. Providing value early in the relationship positions you as a generous and thoughtful contact.

4. A Clear Next Step

If appropriate, suggest a next step—whether it's scheduling a follow-up call, meeting for coffee, or collaborating on a project. A clear call to action keeps the momentum going.

5. Brevity

Keep your follow-up concise. Respect the other person's time by getting to the point quickly while still conveying warmth and sincerity.

Best Practices for Staying Connected

Follow-up isn't a one-time event—it's an ongoing practice. Here are best practices for staying connected with your network over the long term:

1. Create a Follow-Up System

Develop a system to track your contacts and follow-ups. This could be a simple spreadsheet, a CRM tool, or a dedicated app. Record key details about each contact, including when you last communicated, topics discussed, and any commitments you made.

2. Schedule Regular Check-Ins

Set reminders to check in with your contacts periodically. For close connections, this might be monthly; for more distant ones, quarterly or biannually may suffice. Regular check-ins prevent relationships from going stale.

3. Share Relevant Content

Share articles, podcasts, or resources that align with your contacts' interests or goals. This demonstrates that you're thinking of them and positions you as a valuable source of information.

4. Celebrate Milestones

Acknowledge important events in your contacts' lives—promotions, work anniversaries, birthdays, or personal achievements. A quick note of congratulations strengthens the bond and shows you care.

5. Engage on Social Media

Interact with your contacts on platforms like LinkedIn by liking, commenting on, or sharing their posts. This keeps you visible and reinforces your engagement with their professional journey.

6. Offer Help Proactively

Don't wait to be asked. If you come across an opportunity, resource, or connection that might benefit someone in your network, share it. Proactive helpfulness builds enduring goodwill.

7. Be Authentic

Avoid transactional or overly formal follow-ups. Authenticity is key to building real relationships. Write as you would speak, and let your genuine personality shine through.

8. Don't Overdo It

While staying in touch is important, avoid overwhelming your contacts with too many messages. Strike a balance that feels natural and respectful of their time.

Common Follow-Up Mistakes to Avoid

Even with the best intentions, follow-ups can go wrong. Here are some common pitfalls to avoid:

- **Waiting Too Long**: Delayed follow-ups lose their impact. Aim to reach out within 48 hours of an initial meeting.
- **Being Too Generic**: Cookie-cutter messages feel impersonal and are easily dismissed. Always personalize.
- **Focusing Only on Yourself**: Follow-ups that only ask for favors without offering value can damage relationships. Aim for reciprocity.
- **Neglecting Long-Term Connections**: Don't only reach out when you need something. Consistent, no-strings-attached communication is key.
- **Forgetting to Follow Through**: If you promise to send a resource or make an introduction, do it. Broken promises erode trust.

Conclusion

Follow-up is the unsung hero of networking. It's the quiet, consistent effort that turns fleeting introductions into meaningful, lasting relationships. By following up promptly, personally, and with genuine value, you position yourself as a trusted and valued member of your network. Over time, these efforts compound, creating a rich web of connections that support your personal and professional growth.

In the next chapter, we'll explore how to build a diverse network and the benefits of cultivating connections across different demographics, industries, and backgrounds.

Part 4: Understanding Net Worth Chapter 13: Defining Net Worth Assets vs. liabilities: what counts? The importance of tracking your net worth. Chapter 14: Financial Literacy Fundamentals Basic financial concepts everyone should know.

Resources for improving financial literacy. Chapter 15: Creating a Budget and Savings Plan Steps to develop a personal budget. Strategies for saving effectively. Chapter 16: Investing Basics Overview of investment options (stocks, bonds, real estate). Risk assessment and portfolio diversification. Part 5: Increasing Your Net Worth Chapter 17: Income Streams Identifying and creating multiple income sources. Passive income strategies. Chapter 18: Leveraging Networking for Financial Gains How to turn connections into clients or business opportunities. Networking tactics for entrepreneurs. Chapter 19: Building a Personal Development Plan Setting goals for career advancement. Investing in skills and education. Chapter 20: Risk Management and Insurance Importance of protecting your assets. Types of insurance to consider. Part 6: Sustaining Success Chapter 21: Giving Back and Community Engagement The role of philanthropy in networking and net worth. Building a legacy through community involvement. Chapter 22: Adapting to Change Staying relevant in a changing economy. Networking in a digital age. Chapter 23: Continuous Learning and Growth Emphasizing lifelong learning. Resources for ongoing education. Chapter 24: Measuring Your Success Tools for assessing networking and financial growth. Adjusting strategies based on results.

ChatGPT said:

ChatGPT

Chapter 7: Follow-Up Strategies

Networking is an ongoing process, and the connections you make can significantly influence your personal and professional growth. However, the work does not end after an initial meeting or conversation. Effective follow-up strategies are essential to nurturing these connections, keeping the momentum alive, and ensuring that relationships are meaningful and mutually beneficial. In this chapter, we will explore the importance of timely follow-ups and outline best practices for staying connected.

Importance of Timely Follow-Ups

1. Reinforcing Relationships

Timely follow-ups help reinforce the relationship you've started to build. They demonstrate that you value the connection and are interested in maintaining communication. A follow-up can turn a one-time interaction into a lasting relationship.

2. Creating Opportunities

Following up provides opportunities to deepen your relationship and explore potential collaborations. Whether it's sharing resources, discussing ideas, or simply catching up, these interactions can lead to new opportunities for both parties.

3. Staying Top of Mind

Regular follow-ups help keep you and your brand at the forefront of someone's mind. This is particularly important in professional settings, where opportunities often arise based on personal connections. A thoughtful follow-up can make you memorable, increasing the chances that your contact will think of you when an opportunity arises.

Best Practices for Staying Connected

1. Choose the Right Medium

Deciding how to follow up is as important as the content of the follow-up itself. Depending on your relationship and the context of your interaction, you can choose from various mediums:

- **Email**: Ideal for professional follow-ups, allowing for a thoughtful, structured message.
- **Social Media**: Platforms like LinkedIn can be effective for informal connections and quick updates.
- **Phone Calls or Video Chats**: Best for deeper conversations or if you have a strong rapport.

2. Personalize Your Message

A personalized follow-up is much more effective than a generic one. Mention specifics from your previous conversation to jog their memory and show that you were engaged. This can include referencing a shared interest, a project they mentioned, or a piece of advice they offered.

Example:

"Hi [Name], it was great meeting you at [Event]! I really enjoyed our discussion about [specific topic]. I found the resources you mentioned incredibly helpful. Would love to hear more about your project on [related topic]!"

3. Set a Reminder for Follow-Ups

Don't leave follow-ups to memory alone; set reminders to reach out. You can use digital tools, such as calendar apps or CRM software, to schedule reminders for future touchpoints. This helps you stay proactive in maintaining your connections.

4. Share Relevant Content

Another excellent way to follow up is by sharing articles, resources, or information that is relevant to the other person's interests or challenges. This not only adds value but also keeps the conversation going.

Example:

"Hi [Name], I came across this article about [topic of interest] and thought of you. It aligns perfectly with our conversation at [Event]. I hope you find it helpful!"

5. Express Gratitude

Expressing gratitude can go a long way in building rapport. Thank your contacts for their time, insights, or assistance. A simple thank-you message can make them feel appreciated and more inclined to engage with you in the future.

Example:

"Thank you so much for your advice during our last conversation. It really helped me to clarify my approach to [specific issue]."

6. Establish a Follow-Up Schedule

Depending on the depth of your relationship, establish a follow-up schedule that suits both parties. This could be monthly, quarterly, or based on specific milestones. Regular check-ins help ensure that you remain engaged without overwhelming your contacts.

7. Be Mindful of Timing

The timing of your follow-up can greatly impact its effectiveness. Aim to follow up within a few days of your initial interaction while the meeting is still fresh in their mind. However, be considerate of their schedule; if they're busy, allow some space before reaching out again.

Managing Different Types of Follow-Ups

1. After Events or Meetings

Following up after networking events or meetings is crucial. Send a message within 48 hours, referencing the event and your conversation. This shows initiative and reinforces your interest.

2. After a Job Interview or Informational Meeting

If you've had an interview or an informational meeting, a thank-you email is essential. Express appreciation for their time and restate your interest. This not only shows professionalism but also helps keep the lines of communication open.

3. For Long-Term Connections

For contacts you haven't spoken to in a while, a simple "checking in" message can reignite the connection. Share a brief update about yourself and inquire about them. This type of follow-up can remind them of your relationship and re-establish rapport.

Example:

"Hi [Name], I hope you've been well! It's been a while since we last connected, and I'd love to hear how things are going for you. I've been working on [brief update]. Let's catch up soon!"

Conclusion

Effective follow-up strategies are essential for transforming initial networking interactions into meaningful relationships. By being timely, personal, and thoughtful in your follow-ups, you can ensure that your connections remain strong and continue to yield opportunities for growth. In the next chapter, we will discuss building a diverse network, exploring the benefits of diverse connections and strategies for reaching out to different demographics.

4o mini

You said:

Chapter 8: Building a Diverse Network

In an increasingly interconnected and globalized world, the value of a diverse network cannot be overstated. A diverse network is more than a collection of contacts from different backgrounds—it is a dynamic ecosystem of perspectives, experiences, skills, and opportunities that can propel your personal and professional growth to new heights. This chapter explores the profound benefits of diversity in connections and provides actionable strategies for reaching out to different demographics.

The Benefits of Diversity in Connections

When we speak of diversity in networking, we refer to the inclusion of people from various races, ethnicities, genders, ages, sexual orientations, socioeconomic backgrounds, industries, professions, educational levels, geographic locations, and life experiences. A truly diverse network reflects the richness of the world around us and offers countless advantages.

1. Broader Perspectives and Innovative Thinking

One of the most significant benefits of a diverse network is exposure to a wide range of perspectives. When you surround yourself with people who think differently, you challenge your assumptions, expand your worldview, and sharpen your critical thinking. Diverse perspectives are the bedrock of innovation. Studies have consistently shown that diverse teams outperform homogeneous ones in problem-solving, creativity, and decision-making. By connecting with individuals from different walks of life, you gain access to ideas and solutions you may never have considered on your own.

2. Expanded Opportunities

A diverse network opens doors to opportunities that might otherwise remain hidden. Each person in your network operates within their own sphere of influence, with unique access to industries, markets, and communities. By cultivating relationships across demographics, you tap into a broader pool of job openings, business partnerships, investment opportunities, and collaborative projects. Diversity multiplies the possibilities available to you.

3. Enhanced Cultural Competence

In today's global economy, cultural competence is a critical skill. Engaging with people from different cultural backgrounds enhances your ability to communicate, negotiate, and collaborate across cultures. This competence is invaluable whether you are doing business internationally, managing a diverse team, or navigating multicultural communities. A diverse network naturally develops your cultural intelligence and empathy.

4. Resilience and Adaptability

A diverse network makes you more resilient and adaptable. Different perspectives help you anticipate challenges, adjust to change, and recover from setbacks. When one area of your network experiences difficulty, others can offer support, guidance, and alternative pathways forward. Diversity acts as a safety net, providing stability in uncertain times.

5. Personal Growth and Empathy

Beyond professional benefits, a diverse network enriches your personal life. Building meaningful relationships with people unlike yourself fosters empathy, humility, and a deeper understanding of the human experience. You learn to appreciate differences, celebrate commonalities, and grow as a person. This personal growth translates into stronger leadership, better communication, and more fulfilling relationships.

6. Stronger Reputation and Credibility

Being known as someone who values diversity and inclusion enhances your reputation. In an era where organizations and individuals are increasingly judged by their commitment to equity, having a diverse network signals that you are open-minded, forward-thinking, and socially conscious. This reputation can attract like-minded individuals and open doors to leadership roles and influential communities.

Strategies for Reaching Out to Different Demographics

Building a diverse network requires intention, effort, and genuine curiosity. It does not happen by accident. Below are practical strategies to help you intentionally expand your connections across demographics.

1. Audit Your Current Network

Before you can diversify your network, you need to understand its current composition. Take stock of your existing connections. Who are they? What industries do they represent? What backgrounds, ages, and perspectives do they bring? Identifying gaps in your network is the first step toward filling them. Be honest with yourself—most of us unconsciously gravitate toward people similar to us.

2. Step Outside Your Comfort Zone

Diversifying your network requires stepping beyond familiar circles. Attend events, conferences, and gatherings where you are not the majority. Join organizations, professional groups, or community initiatives that cater to people different from you. While it may feel uncomfortable at first, this discomfort is often where the most meaningful growth occurs.

3. Leverage Online Platforms

Digital platforms such as LinkedIn, Twitter, and industry-specific forums make it easier than ever to connect with people worldwide. Follow thought leaders from diverse backgrounds, engage with their content, and initiate conversations. Join online communities, virtual events, and webinars that attract diverse audiences. Be proactive in sending thoughtful connection requests and messages.

4. Seek Out Affinity Groups and Associations

Many professional affinity groups and associations exist to support underrepresented communities. Examples include organizations for women in leadership, minority professionals, LGBTQ+ networks, veterans, and people with disabilities. Engaging with these groups—whether as a member, ally, or supporter—provides access to rich, diverse communities.

5. Be a Lifelong Learner

Approach networking with a learner's mindset. Read books, attend lectures, listen to podcasts, and consume media created by people from different backgrounds. Educating yourself about other cultures, histories, and experiences prepares you to engage authentically and respectfully. It also gives you common ground when initiating conversations.

6. Practice Active Inclusion

Building a diverse network is not just about meeting people; it is about making them feel welcomed and valued. Practice active inclusion by listening attentively, acknowledging different viewpoints, and creating space for others to contribute. Be mindful of biases and microaggressions, and commit to continuous self-improvement.

7. Offer Value First

Networking is a two-way street. When reaching out to new connections, focus on how you can add value rather than what you can gain. Offer your expertise, make introductions, share resources, or simply provide encouragement. Generosity builds trust and lays the foundation for lasting relationships.

8. Engage in Community Service

Volunteering and community service are powerful ways to meet people from diverse backgrounds while contributing to meaningful causes. Whether you mentor youth, participate in charitable initiatives, or support grassroots organizations, these activities connect you with passionate, purpose-driven individuals.

9. Travel and Explore

If possible, travel broadens your horizons and introduces you to people from different cultures and regions. Even local travel—visiting neighborhoods, cultural festivals, or events outside your usual routine—can expose you to new communities. Travel fosters curiosity and creates opportunities for authentic connection.

10. Be Patient and Persistent

Building a diverse network takes time. Relationships are built on trust, consistency, and shared experiences. Be patient with the process and persistent in your efforts. Celebrate small wins and remain committed to your goal of cultivating a rich, diverse network.

Overcoming Challenges in Building a Diverse Network

While the benefits of diversity are clear, the journey is not without challenges. You may encounter unconscious biases—both your own and others'. You may face awkward moments or misunderstandings. You may feel like an outsider in unfamiliar spaces. These challenges are part of the learning process.

Approach them with humility, openness, and a willingness to grow. Seek feedback from trusted friends and mentors. Reflect on your experiences and adjust your approach as needed. Remember that building a diverse network is not about checking boxes or meeting quotas—it is about building genuine, respectful, and mutually beneficial relationships.

Conclusion

A diverse network is one of the most valuable assets you can cultivate in your personal and professional life. It expands your perspectives, opens doors to new opportunities, enhances your cultural competence, and enriches your life in countless ways. By intentionally reaching out to people across demographics, stepping outside your comfort zone, and practicing active inclusion, you build a network that reflects the best of humanity—diverse, dynamic, and deeply connected.

As you move forward in your networking journey, remember that diversity is not just a strategy; it is a mindset. Embrace it fully, and you will find that your network becomes not only broader but also more meaningful, resilient, and impactful. In the next chapter, we will explore how to leverage your network for opportunities, turning your connections into catalysts for success.

Part 4: Understanding Net Worth Chapter 13: Defining Net Worth Assets vs. liabilities: what counts? The importance of tracking your net worth. Chapter 14: Financial Literacy Fundamentals Basic financial concepts everyone should know.

Resources for improving financial literacy. Chapter 15: Creating a Budget and Savings Plan Steps to develop a personal budget. Strategies for saving effectively. Chapter 16: Investing Basics Overview of investment options (stocks, bonds, real estate). Risk assessment and portfolio diversification. Part 5: Increasing Your Net Worth Chapter 17: Income Streams Identifying and creating multiple income sources. Passive income strategies. Chapter 18: Leveraging Networking for Financial Gains How to turn connections into clients or business opportunities. Networking tactics for entrepreneurs. Chapter 19: Building a Personal Development Plan Setting goals for career advancement. Investing in skills and education. Chapter 20: Risk Management and Insurance Importance of protecting your assets. Types of insurance to consider. Part 6: Sustaining Success Chapter 21: Giving Back and Community Engagement The role of philanthropy in networking and net worth. Building a legacy through community involvement. Chapter 22: Adapting to Change Staying relevant in a changing economy. Networking in a digital age. Chapter 23: Continuous Learning and Growth Emphasizing lifelong learning. Resources for ongoing education. Chapter 24: Measuring Your Success Tools for assessing networking and financial growth. Adjusting strategies based on results.

ChatGPT said:

ChatGPT

Chapter 8: Building a Diverse Network

In today's interconnected world, building a diverse network is not just a nicety; it's a necessity. Diversity in your network can lead to richer perspectives, innovative ideas, and greater opportunities. In this chapter, we will explore the benefits of diversity in connections and offer strategies for effectively reaching out to different demographics.

Benefits of Diversity in Connections

1. Enhanced Creativity and Innovation

Diverse networks bring together people with varied backgrounds, experiences, and viewpoints. This diversity fosters creativity and innovation, as individuals approach problems from different angles. Engaging with a wide range of perspectives can lead to breakthrough ideas and solutions that may not emerge within a homogeneous group.

2. Broader Access to Opportunities

A diverse network opens doors to opportunities that you might not encounter within a more uniform group. By connecting with individuals from various fields, cultures, and demographics, you gain insights into different markets, industries, and trends, increasing your chances of identifying unique opportunities.

3. Improved Problem-Solving Skills

When faced with challenges, a diverse network can serve as a valuable resource. Different experiences and viewpoints can help you see issues from multiple angles, leading to more effective problem-solving. Diverse teams are often better equipped to analyze situations and generate innovative solutions.

4. Increased Cultural Competence

Building a diverse network enhances your cultural awareness and sensitivity. Engaging with individuals from various backgrounds helps you develop a deeper understanding of different cultures, customs, and perspectives. This cultural competence is invaluable in today's globalized economy and can improve your ability to connect with clients and colleagues from diverse backgrounds.

5. Stronger Support Systems

A diverse network creates a rich tapestry of support and encouragement. Different individuals can offer varying insights, resources, and encouragement, enhancing your overall support system. When you have a diverse group of connections, you can draw on a wider range of skills and experiences when seeking advice or support.

Strategies for Reaching Out to Different Demographics
1. Identify Your Goals

Before reaching out, clarify your objectives. Are you looking to expand your professional network, learn about a new industry, or gain insights into different cultural perspectives? Knowing your goals will help you target the right demographics and focus your outreach efforts effectively.

2. Utilize Social Media Platforms

Social media is a powerful tool for connecting with diverse individuals. Platforms like LinkedIn, Twitter, and Instagram allow you to engage with people across various industries and backgrounds. Follow thought leaders, join relevant groups, and participate in discussions to expand your network.

3. Attend Inclusive Events

Participate in events that emphasize diversity and inclusion. Conferences, workshops, and community gatherings focused on specific demographics or industries can help you meet individuals you might not encounter in traditional networking settings. Look for events that cater to underrepresented groups or explore topics related to diversity.

4. Engage in Volunteer Work

Volunteering for causes that resonate with you can introduce you to individuals from diverse backgrounds who share similar passions. This not only expands your network but also allows you to contribute positively to your community. Engaging in volunteer work fosters authentic connections built on shared values.

5. Leverage Existing Connections

Reach out to your current network and ask for introductions to individuals from different backgrounds. Personal referrals can ease the way for connections and help establish trust more quickly. When asking for introductions, be clear about why you're interested in connecting and what you hope to gain from the conversation.

6. Participate in Cultural Events

Attending cultural festivals, workshops, and community events can help you connect with individuals from different backgrounds. These events provide a relaxed environment to meet new people, learn about different cultures, and foster relationships based on mutual interests.

7. Be Open-Minded and Respectful

When engaging with individuals from diverse backgrounds, approach the conversation with an open mind and genuine curiosity. Show respect for their experiences and perspectives, even if they differ from your own. Building trust and rapport is essential for developing meaningful connections.

8. Follow Up with Intent

After meeting new contacts, follow up with a personalized message. Express appreciation for the conversation and mention any shared interests or topics discussed. This helps solidify the connection and lays the groundwork for future interactions.

Conclusion

Building a diverse network is a vital strategy for personal and professional growth. The benefits of diverse connections range from enhanced creativity and innovation to broader access to opportunities. By actively seeking to engage with individuals from different demographics, you can enrich your network and position yourself for greater success. In the next chapter, we will explore how to leverage your network to identify and seize opportunities effectively, transforming connections into tangible benefits for your career and personal life.

4o mini

You said:

Chapter 9: Networking for Opportunities

In the journey of personal and professional growth, networking stands as one of the most powerful tools at our disposal. It is not merely about exchanging business cards or connecting on LinkedIn; it is about cultivating relationships that can lead to meaningful opportunities. This chapter delves into how to identify and seize opportunities through your connections, supported by case studies of successful networking that demonstrate the transformative power of a well-maintained network.

Understanding the Landscape of Opportunities

Opportunities can come in many forms — job offers, partnerships, mentorships, investment prospects, or even invitations to collaborate on creative projects. The first step in networking for opportunities is to develop a mindset that recognizes potential in every interaction. Opportunities rarely announce themselves loudly; more often, they whisper through casual conversations, shared interests, or passing mentions of challenges that your skills could solve.

To position yourself to hear these whispers, you must be intentional about three things: clarity regarding what you seek, curiosity about the people you meet, and a willingness to offer value before expecting anything in return. When you approach networking from this place, opportunities emerge organically.

How to Identify Opportunities Through Connections

1. Listen Actively and Purposefully

Most opportunities are hidden in plain sight during conversations. When someone mentions they are struggling to find a qualified candidate, searching for a reliable vendor, or exploring a new market, that is an opportunity — either for you directly or for someone in your network. Train yourself to listen not just for what is being said, but for the underlying needs and aspirations.

2. Map Your Network

Take inventory of your existing connections. Categorize them by industry, expertise, influence, and the nature of your relationship. This map becomes a strategic asset. When opportunities arise, you will know exactly who to approach, and when others need help, you will know who in your network can provide it.

3. Stay Informed

Keep up with industry trends, company news, and the activities of people in your network. Following your contacts on professional platforms, subscribing to relevant newsletters, and attending industry events will keep you in the loop. Being informed allows you to spot opportunities early and act before others.

4. Ask the Right Questions

Powerful questions unlock hidden opportunities. Instead of asking, "What do you do?" try asking, "What are you working on that excites you?" or "What challenges are you facing right now?" These questions invite deeper conversation and reveal areas where you might contribute or collaborate.

5. Be Visible and Accessible

Opportunities flow to those who are known and reachable. Share your work, write about your insights, speak at events, and engage thoughtfully on social platforms. When people know what you do and what you are looking for, they will think of you when relevant opportunities arise.

Seizing Opportunities When They Appear

Identifying an opportunity is only half the battle; seizing it requires courage, preparation, and speed.

- **Act Quickly**: Opportunities have a shelf life. Respond promptly to introductions, invitations, and leads. A delayed response can signal disinterest or unreliability.
- **Prepare Thoroughly**: Before meetings or interviews that stem from networking, do your homework. Understand the person, the company, and the context.
- **Communicate Clearly**: Articulate what you bring to the table and what you hope to achieve. Vague intentions lead to vague results.
- **Follow Through**: If you commit to sending a proposal, making an introduction, or delivering work, honor that commitment. Your reputation is built on reliability.

Case Studies of Successful Networking

Case Study 1: The Coffee Chat That Changed a Career

Sarah, a mid-level marketing professional, attended a local industry meetup where she struck up a conversation with an attendee named James over coffee. Rather than pitching herself, she asked about his work and listened intently as he described his company's struggle to revamp their digital strategy. Sarah shared a few thoughtful insights based on her experience. Two weeks later, James reached out with a job offer for a newly created senior role — one that aligned perfectly with Sarah's aspirations. The opportunity arose not because Sarah asked for a job, but because she demonstrated value and genuine interest.

Case Study 2: The Power of a Warm Introduction

Raj, an entrepreneur developing a fintech startup, had been trying unsuccessfully to reach a prominent investor for months. During a casual dinner with a former colleague, he mentioned his challenge. The colleague, who happened to have gone to university with the investor, offered to make an introduction. Within a week, Raj had a meeting scheduled, and within three months, his startup had secured seed funding. The lesson: your network's network is often more valuable than your own direct contacts.

Case Study 3: Collaboration Born From a Conference

Maria, a graphic designer, attended a design conference where she met Daniel, a software developer, during a workshop. They stayed in touch casually over the following year, exchanging occasional messages about projects. When Maria was approached by a client needing both design and development work, she brought Daniel on board. The collaboration was so successful that they eventually launched a joint consultancy, serving clients neither could have attracted alone.

Case Study 4: The Mentor Who Opened Doors

David, a recent graduate, cultivated a relationship with a senior executive he met through an alumni event. Over several months, he sought the executive's advice, shared updates on his progress, and expressed gratitude for the guidance. When a coveted position opened up at a major firm, the executive personally recommended David. The opportunity was not requested — it was earned through consistent, respectful engagement.

Key Takeaways

Networking for opportunities is both an art and a discipline. It requires patience, authenticity, and a long-term perspective. The most successful networkers are not those who collect the most contacts, but those who build the deepest relationships and consistently add value to others. By listening actively, staying informed, asking powerful questions, and acting with integrity, you position yourself to recognize and seize opportunities that others might overlook.

Remember: every person you meet is a potential doorway to possibilities you cannot yet imagine. Treat each connection with respect and curiosity, and the opportunities will follow.

Part 4: Understanding Net Worth Chapter 13: Defining Net Worth Assets vs. liabilities: what counts? The importance of tracking your net worth. Chapter 14: Financial Literacy Fundamentals Basic financial concepts everyone should know.

Resources for improving financial literacy. Chapter 15: Creating a Budget and Savings Plan Steps to develop a personal budget. Strategies for saving effectively. Chapter 16: Investing Basics Overview of investment options (stocks, bonds, real estate). Risk assessment and portfolio diversification. Part 5: Increasing Your Net Worth Chapter 17: Income Streams Identifying and creating multiple income sources. Passive income strategies. Chapter 18: Leveraging Networking for Financial Gains How to turn connections into clients or business opportunities. Networking tactics for entrepreneurs. Chapter 19: Building a Personal Development Plan Setting goals for career advancement. Investing in skills and education. Chapter 20: Risk Management and Insurance Importance of protecting your assets. Types of insurance to consider. Part 6: Sustaining Success Chapter 21: Giving Back and Community Engagement The role of philanthropy in networking and net worth. Building a legacy through community involvement. Chapter 22: Adapting to Change Staying relevant in a changing economy. Networking in a digital age. Chapter 23: Continuous Learning and Growth Emphasizing lifelong learning. Resources for ongoing education. Chapter 24: Measuring Your Success Tools for assessing networking and financial growth. Adjusting strategies based on results.

ChatGPT said:

ChatGPT

Chapter 9: Networking for Opportunities

Networking is not merely a social endeavor; it is a powerful tool for unlocking opportunities that can significantly impact your personal and professional growth. In this chapter, we will explore how to identify and seize opportunities through your connections. We will also examine case studies of successful networking, illustrating how strategic relationships can lead to tangible benefits.

Identifying Opportunities Through Networking

1. Know What You're Looking For

Before diving into networking events or engaging with contacts, clarify the types of opportunities you wish to pursue. Whether you're seeking a job, mentorship, collaboration, or business leads, having a clear focus will help guide your conversations and networking efforts.

2. Tap into Industry Insights

Engage with individuals who are knowledgeable in your field. These connections can provide valuable insights into emerging trends, challenges, and opportunities within the industry. Asking questions and expressing genuine interest can lead to discussions about potential opportunities that align with your goals.

3. Leverage Informational Interviews

Informational interviews are a strategic way to gather insights while building connections. Approach professionals in your network and request short conversations to learn more about their career paths and experiences. These discussions can lead to unexpected opportunities, referrals, or collaborations.

4. Be Open to Unexpected Leads

Opportunities often arise in unexpected places. Be receptive to diverse conversations and be curious about others' experiences. You never know when a casual chat might lead to a significant business opportunity or a new professional relationship.

5. Utilize Social Media for Opportunity Tracking

Platforms like LinkedIn, Twitter, and industry-specific forums can be instrumental in uncovering opportunities. Follow industry leaders, engage with their content, and participate in discussions. Being active in online communities can enhance your visibility and position you as a knowledgeable resource, attracting potential opportunities.

Seizing Opportunities Through Networking

1. Maintain Regular Communication

Once you've identified potential opportunities, stay in touch with your contacts. Regular communication helps reinforce relationships and keeps you top of mind when opportunities arise. Utilize follow-ups, newsletters, or social media interactions to stay engaged.

2. Be Proactive in Offering Help

Networking is a two-way street. When you offer assistance to your connections, you build goodwill and create a supportive network. By being proactive, you increase the likelihood that your contacts will reciprocate when opportunities arise.

3. Create Value Through Content Sharing

Share relevant articles, insights, or resources with your network. Providing value enhances your reputation and positions you as a thought leader. This approach can also spark conversations that lead to new opportunities.

4. Leverage Networking Events for Direct Connections

Networking events provide an excellent platform for meeting potential collaborators, mentors, or clients. Approach these gatherings with a clear strategy. Prepare your elevator pitch, engage in meaningful conversations, and don't hesitate to follow up after the event to solidify the connections.

5. Stay Adaptable and Open-Minded

In networking, adaptability is key. Be willing to pivot and explore opportunities that may differ from your initial goals. Sometimes the most rewarding connections come from unexpected directions.

Case Studies of Successful Networking

Case Study 1: The Career Catalyst

Emily, a recent college graduate, attended a professional conference where she networked with industry leaders. She struck up a conversation with a panelist during a Q&A session, expressing her interest in their work. After the event, she followed up with a thank-you email and requested an informational interview.

During their conversation, Emily learned about an internship opportunity at the panelist's company, which led to her landing a full-time position after completing her internship. Emily's proactive approach and genuine interest in her contacts' work opened doors to her career.

Case Study 2: The Collaborative Entrepreneur

Mark, a small business owner, sought to expand his clientele. He attended local networking events and regularly met with fellow entrepreneurs. After establishing relationships, Mark proposed a collaborative marketing campaign with another business owner he met.

The collaboration resulted in shared resources and increased visibility for both businesses, significantly boosting their customer bases. Mark's willingness to leverage his network for mutual benefit transformed his business trajectory.

Case Study 3: The Power of Mentorship

Jessica, an aspiring writer, was struggling to find her voice in the industry. After attending a writer's workshop, she connected with a seasoned author who offered to mentor her. Through their meetings, Jessica received feedback on her work and learned about publishing opportunities.

With her mentor's guidance, Jessica secured a book deal within a year, showcasing the transformative power of mentorship within a network. Her proactive approach in seeking mentorship exemplified how networking can lead to significant career advancements.

Conclusion

Networking is a strategic approach to identifying and seizing opportunities that can propel your career and personal growth. By actively engaging with your network, maintaining relationships, and being open to unexpected connections, you position yourself for success. The case studies presented illustrate the diverse pathways that effective networking can create, reinforcing the idea that opportunities often arise from the connections you nurture. In the next chapter, we will explore the importance of mentorship and guidance in leveraging your network for personal and professional growth.

Chapter 10: Mentorship and Guidance

Mentorship is one of the most powerful catalysts for personal and professional growth. Within the broader context of networking, mentor-mentee relationships stand apart because they go beyond casual connections—they involve deep investment, trust, and the intentional exchange of wisdom. In this chapter, we'll explore how to find mentors, nurture these relationships, and understand the transformative role mentorship plays in shaping your journey toward mastering network and net worth.

The Role of Mentorship in Personal Growth

A mentor is more than an advisor. They are a guide, a sounding board, a challenger, and often a source of inspiration. Mentorship provides something that books, courses, and even general networking cannot: personalized, experience-based guidance tailored to your unique circumstances.

The benefits of mentorship include:

- **Accelerated Learning:** Mentors help you avoid common pitfalls by sharing lessons they've already learned the hard way.
- **Expanded Perspective:** A mentor challenges your assumptions and introduces you to new ways of thinking.
- **Access to Opportunities:** Mentors often open doors—introductions, recommendations, and invitations that would otherwise remain closed.
- **Accountability:** Regular check-ins with a mentor keep you focused on your goals and committed to progress.
- **Confidence Building:** Knowing that someone experienced believes in your potential can be a powerful motivator.

Mentorship isn't a one-way street. While mentees gain guidance, mentors often find renewed purpose, fresh perspectives, and the satisfaction of contributing to someone else's success.

Finding the Right Mentor

Identifying a mentor requires clarity about what you want to achieve and who can help you get there. Here are steps to guide your search:

1. **Define Your Goals.** Before seeking a mentor, be clear about the areas where you need guidance—career advancement, entrepreneurship, leadership, personal development, or industry expertise.

2. **Look Within Your Existing Network.** Often, potential mentors are already in your orbit—former managers, professors, colleagues, or industry peers you admire.

3. **Attend Industry Events.** Conferences, seminars, and professional associations are fertile ground for meeting seasoned professionals who may become mentors.

4. **Leverage Online Platforms.** LinkedIn, mentorship apps, and professional groups make it easier than ever to connect with experienced individuals across industries.

5. **Seek Diversity.** Don't limit yourself to one mentor. Different mentors can provide insight into different aspects of your life—career, finances, leadership, personal growth.

6. **Evaluate Compatibility.** A good mentor shares values that resonate with yours, communicates in ways you understand, and is genuinely invested in your success.

Approaching a Potential Mentor

Asking someone to be your mentor can feel intimidating, but the key is authenticity and respect for their time. Consider these approaches:

- **Start Small.** Instead of asking someone outright to be your mentor, request a short informational conversation. Build rapport before formalizing the relationship.
- **Be Specific.** Explain why you admire their work and what you hope to learn. Vague requests are easy to decline; specific ones invite engagement.
- **Respect Their Time.** Propose a clear, manageable commitment—perhaps a 30-minute call once a month.
- **Show Initiative.** Come prepared with questions, updates, and reflections. Mentors value mentees who take ownership of their growth.

Nurturing the Mentor-Mentee Relationship

Once a mentorship begins, the responsibility for maintaining it rests largely with the mentee. To cultivate a meaningful and lasting relationship:

- **Be Consistent.** Schedule regular check-ins and honor them.
- **Listen Actively.** Absorb the advice offered, even when it challenges you.
- **Act on Advice.** Nothing frustrates a mentor more than a mentee who never implements guidance. Show progress between meetings.
- **Express Gratitude.** A simple thank-you note or acknowledgment of their impact goes a long way.
- **Give Back.** Even as a mentee, you can offer value—share articles, introduce them to relevant contacts, or celebrate their achievements.

Becoming a Mentor Yourself

As you grow, consider stepping into the mentor role. Mentoring others not only reinforces your own knowledge but also strengthens your network and legacy. Being a mentor signals leadership, builds credibility, and expands your influence.

Effective mentors:

- Listen more than they speak.
- Ask questions that provoke reflection.
- Share stories and experiences, not just advice.
- Encourage independence rather than dependence.
- Celebrate their mentee's wins as their own.

The Ripple Effect of Mentorship

Mentorship creates a ripple effect. Every mentee who grows under guidance becomes capable of mentoring others in turn. This chain of influence is one of the most powerful forces in professional and personal development. By investing in mentor-mentee relationships, you're not just advancing your own journey—you're contributing to a larger culture of growth, generosity, and shared success.

Key Takeaways

- Mentorship accelerates growth by providing personalized, experience-driven guidance.
- Finding the right mentor requires clarity of goals and thoughtful outreach.
- Nurturing the relationship depends on consistency, gratitude, and action.
- Becoming a mentor yourself multiplies your impact and strengthens your network.
- Mentorship is both a gift received and a gift given—a cornerstone of mastering network and net worth.

Part 4: Understanding Net Worth Chapter 13: Defining Net Worth Assets vs. liabilities: what counts? The importance of tracking your net worth. Chapter 14: Financial Literacy Fundamentals Basic financial concepts everyone should know.

Resources for improving financial literacy. Chapter 15: Creating a Budget and Savings Plan Steps to develop a personal budget. Strategies for saving effectively. Chapter 16: Investing Basics Overview of investment options (stocks, bonds, real estate). Risk assessment and portfolio diversification. Part 5: Increasing Your Net Worth Chapter 17: Income Streams Identifying and creating multiple income sources. Passive income strategies. Chapter 18: Leveraging Networking for Financial Gains How to turn connections into clients or business opportunities. Networking tactics for entrepreneurs. Chapter 19: Building a Personal Development Plan Setting goals for career advancement. Investing in skills and education. Chapter 20: Risk Management and Insurance Importance of protecting your assets. Types of insurance to consider. Part 6: Sustaining Success Chapter 21: Giving Back and Community Engagement The role of philanthropy in networking and net worth. Building a legacy through community involvement. Chapter 22: Adapting to Change Staying relevant in a changing economy. Networking in a digital age. Chapter 23: Continuous Learning and Growth Emphasizing lifelong learning. Resources for ongoing education. Chapter 24: Measuring Your Success Tools for assessing networking and financial growth. Adjusting strategies based on results.

ChatGPT said:

ChatGPT

Chapter 10: Mentorship and Guidance

In the journey of personal and professional growth, mentorship plays a pivotal role. The guidance of an experienced mentor can open doors, provide invaluable insights, and help you navigate challenges more effectively. This chapter explores how to find, nurture, and maximize mentor-mentee relationships to enhance your network and, ultimately, your net worth.

Understanding Mentorship

1. Defining Mentorship

Mentorship is a dynamic relationship in which a more experienced individual (the mentor) offers guidance, support, and knowledge to a less experienced individual (the mentee). This relationship can take many forms, including informal friendships, structured programs, or industry-specific mentorship initiatives.

2. The Benefits of Mentorship

- **Knowledge Transfer**: Mentors provide insights that can accelerate your learning curve, allowing you to avoid common pitfalls and make informed decisions.
- **Networking Opportunities**: A mentor can introduce you to their professional network, offering you access to new connections and potential opportunities.
- **Accountability and Support**: Having a mentor can keep you accountable for your goals, providing motivation and encouragement during challenging times.
- **Personal Growth**: Beyond professional development, mentors often help you cultivate important soft skills, such as communication, leadership, and resilience.

Finding the Right Mentor

1. Identify Your Goals

Before seeking a mentor, clarify your objectives. Are you looking to advance in your career, transition to a new field, or develop specific skills? Understanding your goals will help you identify potential mentors who align with your aspirations.

2. Research Potential Mentors

Look for individuals in your field who have achieved what you aspire to do. Utilize LinkedIn, industry associations, or professional networks to identify potential mentors. Pay attention to their experience, expertise, and values to ensure a good fit.

3. Make the Approach

Once you've identified potential mentors, reach out with a clear and respectful message. Introduce yourself, express your admiration for their work, and explain why you would like to connect. Be specific about your goals and what you hope to gain from the relationship.

4. Utilize Networking Events

Attending industry events, conferences, and seminars can provide opportunities to meet potential mentors. Engage in meaningful conversations and express genuine interest in their work to foster a connection.

Nurturing the Mentor-Mentee Relationship

1. Establish Clear Expectations

At the beginning of your mentorship, discuss your goals, preferred communication styles, and how often you'd like to meet. Setting clear expectations will help ensure a productive relationship.

2. Be Open to Feedback

Mentors offer valuable insights based on their experiences. Be receptive to constructive criticism and use it as a tool for growth. This openness fosters a deeper level of trust and respect.

3. Show Appreciation

Acknowledge your mentor's time and effort by expressing gratitude for their guidance. A simple thank-you note or follow-up message after meetings can go a long way in building a positive rapport.

4. Share Your Progress

Regularly update your mentor on your achievements, challenges, and any changes in your goals. This not only keeps them engaged but also allows them to provide relevant advice and support.

The Role of Mentorship in Personal Growth

1. Skill Development

Mentors can help you identify skill gaps and suggest ways to improve. Whether it's enhancing technical skills or developing emotional intelligence, their guidance can shape your personal and professional development.

2. Navigating Career Transitions

If you're considering a career change or advancement, a mentor can offer insights into the industry landscape, help you understand the skills required, and provide guidance on how to position yourself effectively.

3. Building Confidence

Having a mentor can boost your confidence, especially when facing new challenges. Their encouragement and belief in your abilities can empower you to take risks and step out of your comfort zone.

Case Studies of Successful Mentorship

Case Study 1: The Corporate Climb

Sara, a young professional, was struggling to find her footing in a large corporation. She sought out a mentor within the company, a senior executive with a wealth of experience. Through regular meetings, Sara gained insights into corporate culture, learned strategic decision-making, and developed her leadership skills. With her mentor's guidance, she secured a promotion within a year, illustrating the impact of effective mentorship on career advancement.

Case Study 2: The Entrepreneurial Journey

James, an aspiring entrepreneur, was uncertain about launching his startup. He connected with a seasoned entrepreneur through a networking event. Their mentorship relationship flourished, with James receiving guidance on business planning, funding strategies, and market research. As a result, James successfully launched his startup, crediting his mentor for the critical support and advice that made it possible.

Conclusion

Mentorship is a powerful tool that can significantly influence your personal and professional growth. By actively seeking and nurturing mentor-mentee relationships, you not only expand your network but also gain invaluable guidance that propels you toward your goals. As you progress in your journey, remember that mentorship is a reciprocal relationship; by giving back to your mentor and eventually becoming a mentor yourself, you contribute to the cycle of growth and opportunity in your network. In the next chapter, we will explore collaborative networking and how partnerships can yield mutual benefits for all parties involved.

4o mini

You said:

Chapter 11: Collaborative Networking

Building Partnerships for Mutual Benefit

In an increasingly interconnected world, the power of collaboration cannot be overstated. Collaborative networking goes beyond the traditional exchange of business cards and casual introductions; it is about building meaningful partnerships that foster mutual growth, shared success, and long-term value. This chapter explores the principles of collaborative networking, strategies for building effective partnerships, and real-world examples of successful collaborations.

Understanding Collaborative Networking

Collaborative networking is the intentional practice of forming alliances with individuals, organizations, or groups to achieve shared goals. Unlike transactional networking, which often focuses on what one can gain from a connection, collaborative networking emphasizes reciprocity, trust, and long-term value creation. It is rooted in the belief that when people work together, they can accomplish far more than they could alone.

At its core, collaborative networking involves:

- **Shared Vision:** Partners align around common goals or values.
- **Mutual Benefit:** Each party contributes and gains something of value.
- **Trust and Transparency:** Open communication and honesty form the foundation.
- **Complementary Strengths:** Partners bring unique skills, resources, or perspectives to the table.

The Benefits of Collaborative Networking

Collaborative networking offers numerous advantages for individuals and organizations alike:

1. **Expanded Reach:** Partnerships allow you to tap into new audiences, markets, and communities that may have been inaccessible on your own.
2. **Resource Sharing:** Collaborators can pool resources such as expertise, funding, technology, and time, reducing costs and increasing efficiency.
3. **Innovation and Creativity:** Diverse perspectives spark new ideas and solutions, driving innovation.
4. **Risk Mitigation:** Sharing responsibilities and challenges reduces the burden on any single party.
5. **Enhanced Credibility:** Aligning with reputable partners can boost your own credibility and visibility.
6. **Accelerated Growth:** Collaborations often lead to faster achievement of goals, whether launching a product, entering a market, or scaling an initiative.

Principles for Building Successful Partnerships

Building partnerships that stand the test of time requires intentionality and care. Here are key principles to guide your collaborative networking efforts:

1. Identify the Right Partners

Not every connection is suited for collaboration. Look for partners who share your values, complement your strengths, and are committed to mutual success. Consider factors such as:

- Alignment of goals and vision
- Compatibility of working styles
- Reputation and track record
- Willingness to invest time and effort

2. Establish Clear Objectives

Before entering into a partnership, define what you hope to achieve together. Set clear, measurable goals and outline the roles, responsibilities, and expectations of each party. A written agreement or memorandum of understanding can help prevent misunderstandings down the road.

3. Foster Open Communication

Effective communication is the lifeblood of any partnership. Establish regular check-ins, create channels for feedback, and encourage honest dialogue. Address conflicts promptly and constructively to maintain trust and momentum.

4. Contribute Generously

Successful collaborations thrive on generosity. Be willing to share your resources, knowledge, and connections without always expecting immediate returns. Giving freely builds goodwill and strengthens the partnership over time.

5. Celebrate Wins Together

Acknowledge and celebrate milestones, both big and small. Recognizing shared achievements reinforces the value of the partnership and motivates continued collaboration.

6. Evaluate and Evolve

Periodically assess the partnership's progress and impact. Are the goals being met? Is the relationship still mutually beneficial? Be open to evolving the collaboration as circumstances change, or gracefully concluding it when it has run its course.

Strategies for Building Collaborative Partnerships

Here are practical strategies to help you cultivate meaningful collaborations:

- **Attend Industry Events:** Conferences, workshops, and seminars are excellent venues for meeting potential collaborators who share your interests.
- **Join Professional Associations:** Membership in industry groups provides access to like-minded professionals and opportunities for joint initiatives.
- **Leverage Online Platforms:** Use LinkedIn, industry forums, and collaborative tools to connect with potential partners beyond your immediate geographic area.
- **Host Collaborative Events:** Organize webinars, panel discussions, or co-branded events to bring potential partners together.
- **Offer Value First:** Approach potential collaborators with a clear proposition of what you can offer, rather than focusing solely on what you need.
- **Build a Diverse Network:** Seek partners from different industries, backgrounds, and perspectives to enrich your collaborations.

Examples of Successful Collaborations

Real-world examples illustrate the power of collaborative networking:

1. Nike and Apple

The partnership between Nike and Apple is a classic example of collaborative networking. By combining Nike's expertise in athletic apparel with Apple's technology prowess, the two companies launched the Nike+iPod product line, which allowed runners to track their performance through their iPods. This collaboration not only expanded both brands' reach but also set a new standard for wearable fitness technology.

2. Starbucks and Spotify

Starbucks and Spotify joined forces to create a unique in-store music experience. Starbucks employees gained access to Spotify's music library, enabling them to curate playlists for their stores. In return, Spotify gained exposure to Starbucks' vast customer base. This partnership enhanced the customer experience while driving value for both brands.

3. Local Small Business Collaborations

On a smaller scale, local businesses often collaborate to mutual benefit. For example, a bakery and a coffee shop in the same neighborhood might cross-promote each other's products, host joint events, or offer bundled discounts. These grassroots collaborations strengthen community ties and drive customer loyalty.

4. Nonprofit Partnerships

Nonprofits frequently collaborate to amplify their impact. For instance, organizations focused on education, health, and economic empowerment might partner to address the interconnected challenges facing underserved communities. By pooling resources and expertise, they can deliver more comprehensive solutions.

Overcoming Challenges in Collaborative Networking

While collaborative networking offers many rewards, it also comes with challenges. Common obstacles include:

- **Misaligned Expectations:** Differences in goals, priorities, or working styles can create friction.
- **Communication Breakdowns:** Poor communication can lead to misunderstandings and missed opportunities.
- **Unequal Contributions:** Imbalances in effort or resources can breed resentment.
- **External Pressures:** Market changes, organizational shifts, or personal circumstances can strain partnerships.

To navigate these challenges, prioritize transparency, flexibility, and a commitment to problem-solving. Remember that every partnership is a learning opportunity, and even unsuccessful collaborations can yield valuable lessons.

Conclusion

Collaborative networking is a powerful approach to building a rich, resilient, and rewarding network. By focusing on mutual benefit, shared vision, and long-term value, you can create partnerships that drive personal and professional growth. Whether you're a seasoned professional or just beginning your networking journey, embracing collaboration will open doors to opportunities you never imagined possible.

As you move forward, remember that the strength of your network is not measured by the number of connections you have, but by the depth and quality of the partnerships you cultivate. Invest in collaborative networking, and watch as your network—and your net worth—grow in ways that are both meaningful and lasting.

Part 4: Understanding Net Worth

Chapter 13: Defining Net Worth

Assets vs. liabilities: what counts?
The importance of tracking your net worth.

Chapter 14: Financial Literacy Fundamentals

Basic financial concepts everyone should know.
Resources for improving financial literacy.

Chapter 15: Creating a Budget and Savings Plan

Steps to develop a personal budget.
Strategies for saving effectively.

Chapter 16: Investing Basics

Overview of investment options (stocks, bonds, real estate).
Risk assessment and portfolio diversification.

Part 5: Increasing Your Net Worth

Chapter 17: Income Streams

Identifying and creating multiple income sources.
Passive income strategies.

Chapter 18: Leveraging Networking for Financial Gains

How to turn connections into clients or business opportunities.
Networking tactics for entrepreneurs.

Chapter 19: Building a Personal Development Plan

Setting goals for career advancement.
Investing in skills and education.

Chapter 20: Risk Management and Insurance

Importance of protecting your assets.
Types of insurance to consider.

Part 6: Sustaining Success

Chapter 21: Giving Back and Community Engagement

The role of philanthropy in networking and net worth.
Building a legacy through community involvement.

Chapter 22: Adapting to Change

Staying relevant in a changing economy.
Networking in a digital age.

Chapter 23: Continuous Learning and Growth

Emphasizing lifelong learning.
Resources for ongoing education.

Chapter 24: Measuring Your Success

Tools for assessing networking and financial growth.
Adjusting strategies based on results.

ChatGPT said:

ChatGPT

Chapter 11: Collaborative Networking

In a world where collaboration is becoming increasingly vital, the ability to build partnerships for mutual benefit can significantly enhance your network and net worth. This chapter explores the principles of collaborative networking, the advantages it offers, and practical strategies to foster and sustain successful collaborations.

Understanding Collaborative Networking
1. What is Collaborative Networking?

Collaborative networking involves forming alliances with others to achieve shared goals or to leverage each other's strengths. It transcends traditional networking by emphasizing cooperation and reciprocity rather than mere transactional relationships. This approach not only enhances your network but also creates opportunities for innovation, resource sharing, and personal growth.

2. The Value of Collaboration

- **Shared Resources**: Collaboration allows you to pool resources, whether it's knowledge, contacts, or financial support, maximizing potential outcomes.
- **Diverse Perspectives**: Engaging with diverse individuals brings new ideas and approaches, fostering creativity and innovation.
- **Increased Opportunities**: Collaborating with others can expose you to new markets, clients, and projects that you might not reach independently.
- **Supportive Environment**: A collaborative network provides emotional and professional support, enhancing resilience and motivation.

Building Effective Collaborations

1. Identify Potential Collaborators

To build effective collaborations, begin by identifying individuals or organizations whose goals align with yours. Look for:

- **Complementary Skills**: Seek out those who possess skills or expertise that complement your own.
- **Shared Values**: Find partners who share your values and vision to ensure a harmonious working relationship.
- **Common Goals**: Collaborators should have similar objectives to foster mutual benefit.

2. Engage and Initiate Conversations

Once potential collaborators are identified, initiate conversations to explore possibilities. Use these strategies:

- **Leverage Existing Connections**: Reach out through mutual contacts to establish trust and facilitate introductions.
- **Attend Networking Events**: Participate in events relevant to your field, and engage in discussions to identify shared interests.
- **Utilize Online Platforms**: Use social media and professional networks like LinkedIn to connect with potential collaborators.

3. Establish Clear Objectives

Once a collaboration is in the works, establish clear objectives and expectations. Consider:

- **Defining Roles**: Clearly outline each party's responsibilities to prevent misunderstandings.
- **Setting Measurable Goals**: Create specific, measurable goals that will allow you to track progress and success.
- **Communicating Regularly**: Maintain open lines of communication to discuss progress, address concerns, and adapt as necessary.

Maintaining Collaborative Relationships
1. Foster Trust and Respect

Trust is the foundation of any successful collaboration. To foster trust:

- **Be Transparent**: Openly share your ideas, progress, and any challenges you encounter.
- **Honor Commitments**: Follow through on your promises and deliver on your commitments.
- **Celebrate Achievements**: Acknowledge and celebrate both individual and collective achievements to build camaraderie.

2. Encourage Feedback

Regular feedback helps strengthen collaborations and improve outcomes. Encourage a culture of constructive criticism by:

- **Creating a Safe Space**: Foster an environment where partners feel comfortable sharing feedback without fear of repercussion.
- **Being Receptive**: Show willingness to accept feedback and make adjustments as needed.
- **Offering Support**: Provide constructive feedback to your collaborators, helping them grow and succeed.

3. Adapt and Evolve

Collaborations may require adjustments over time due to changing circumstances or goals. To stay relevant:

- **Review Objectives Regularly**: Periodically assess the partnership's goals and adjust as necessary to ensure alignment.
- **Be Open to Change**: Embrace new ideas and approaches that may arise from discussions with collaborators.
- **Expand the Network**: As your collaboration grows, consider bringing in additional partners to enhance capabilities and resources.

Case Studies of Successful Collaborative Networking

Case Study 1: Tech Startups Unite

A group of tech startups, each specializing in different aspects of digital marketing, formed a collaborative network to tackle larger clients. By pooling their resources and expertise, they offered comprehensive solutions, combining SEO, content marketing, and social media management. This collaboration not only increased their individual client bases but also positioned them as a formidable player in the market.

Case Study 2: Community-Based Health Initiatives

In a small town, local health professionals, fitness trainers, and nutritionists collaborated to launch a community health initiative. By combining their expertise, they created a series of workshops and events promoting healthy lifestyles. This initiative not only improved community health but also increased visibility for each professional involved, leading to new clients and partnerships.

Conclusion

Collaborative networking is a powerful strategy for expanding your reach and maximizing your impact. By building partnerships that are grounded in mutual benefit, you not only enhance your network but also create opportunities for growth and innovation. As you embrace the principles of collaboration, remember that the strength of your network lies in the connections you build and the value you create together. In the next chapter, we will delve into the important aspects of networking etiquette, helping you navigate the dos and don'ts of professional networking to ensure lasting relationships.

4o mini

You said:

write chapter 12 for the book Mastering Network and Net Worth Chapter 1: Understanding Networking Definition and significance of networking. Different types of networks (personal, professional, social). Chapter 2: The Psychology of Networking Building trust and rapport. Overcoming networking anxiety. Chapter 3: Identifying Your Networking Goals Assessing personal and professional aspirations. Setting measurable networking objectives. Chapter 4: Building Your Personal Brand Crafting your personal story. Importance of online presence (LinkedIn, social media). Part 2: Expanding Your Network Chapter 5: Where to Network Identifying key networking opportunities (conferences, seminars, online platforms). Leveraging community events and local groups. Chapter 6: The Art of Conversation Effective communication skills. Active listening and engagement techniques. Chapter 7: Follow-Up Strategies Importance of timely follow-ups. Best practices for staying connected. Chapter 8: Building a Diverse Network Benefits of diversity in connections. Strategies for reaching out to different demographics. Part 3: Leveraging Your Network for Success Chapter 9: Networking for Opportunities How to identify and seize opportunities through connections. Case studies of successful networking. Chapter 10: Mentorship and Guidance Finding and nurturing mentor-mentee relationships. The role of mentorship in personal growth. Chapter 11: Collaborative Networking Building partnerships for mutual benefit. Examples of successful collaborations. Chapter 12: Networking Etiquette Dos and don'ts of professional networking. Navigating cultural differences in networking.

Part 4: Understanding Net Worth Chapter 13: Defining Net Worth Assets vs. liabilities: what counts? The importance of tracking your net worth. Chapter 14: Financial Literacy Fundamentals Basic financial concepts everyone should know.

Resources for improving financial literacy. Chapter 15: Creating a Budget and Savings Plan Steps to develop a personal budget. Strategies for saving effectively. Chapter 16: Investing Basics Overview of investment options (stocks, bonds, real estate). Risk assessment and portfolio diversification. Part 5: Increasing Your Net Worth Chapter 17: Income Streams Identifying and creating multiple income sources. Passive income strategies. Chapter 18: Leveraging Networking for Financial Gains How to turn connections into clients or business opportunities. Networking tactics for entrepreneurs. Chapter 19: Building a Personal Development Plan Setting goals for career advancement. Investing in skills and education. Chapter 20: Risk Management and Insurance Importance of protecting your assets. Types of insurance to consider. Part 6: Sustaining Success Chapter 21: Giving Back and Community Engagement The role of philanthropy in networking and net worth. Building a legacy through community involvement. Chapter 22: Adapting to Change Staying relevant in a changing economy. Networking in a digital age. Chapter 23: Continuous Learning and Growth Emphasizing lifelong learning. Resources for ongoing education. Chapter 24: Measuring Your Success Tools for assessing networking and financial growth. Adjusting strategies based on results.

ChatGPT said:

ChatGPT

Chapter 12: Networking Etiquette

Networking is a vital skill for personal and professional growth, but its effectiveness relies heavily on understanding and practicing proper etiquette. The way you interact with others can significantly influence your relationships, opportunities, and reputation. This chapter will provide you with a comprehensive overview of networking etiquette, highlighting essential dos and don'ts, and offering strategies for navigating cultural differences in networking.

The Dos of Networking Etiquette

1. Be Respectful of Time

Respecting others' time is a fundamental aspect of networking etiquette. This means:

- **Arriving on Time**: Always arrive at networking events, meetings, or casual meet-ups on time. If you're running late, communicate your delay as soon as possible.
- **Keeping Conversations Concise**: Be mindful of the time you take during discussions. Aim for concise communication that conveys your message without overwhelming the other person.

2. Practice Active Listening

Active listening is crucial for building rapport and understanding. Here's how to engage effectively:

- **Make Eye Contact**: This shows that you are attentive and interested in what the other person is saying.
- **Ask Open-Ended Questions**: Encourage the other person to share more about themselves or their work, fostering deeper conversations.
- **Avoid Interrupting**: Allow the speaker to finish their thoughts before responding. This demonstrates respect and consideration.

3. Be Authentic

Authenticity builds trust and fosters genuine connections. To maintain authenticity:

- **Be Yourself**: Don't try to put on a façade or present an exaggerated version of yourself. People appreciate honesty.
- **Share Personal Stories**: Relate your experiences and values to create a more personal connection.

4. Follow Up

Timely follow-ups are crucial to reinforcing connections. Here's how to do it right:

- **Send a Thank-You Note**: After meeting someone, send a brief thank-you email or message expressing your gratitude for their time and insights.
- **Connect on Social Media**: If appropriate, send a request on LinkedIn or other relevant platforms to maintain the connection.
- **Offer Value**: In your follow-up, mention something of value to them—an article, a resource, or a suggestion for further discussion.

The Don'ts of Networking Etiquette

1. Avoid Being Overly Aggressive

While it's important to be proactive, being overly aggressive can be off-putting. Avoid:

- **Pushing for Immediate Gains**: Don't expect immediate favors or business; networking is about building relationships over time.
- **Selling Too Hard**: Instead of using every conversation as a sales pitch, focus on relationship-building first.

2. Don't Monopolize Conversations

Networking is a two-way street. To ensure balanced interactions:

- **Encourage Others to Speak**: Allow others to share their thoughts and experiences without dominating the conversation.
- **Be Attentive to Body Language**: If someone seems disengaged or is trying to exit the conversation, gracefully wrap it up.

3. Refrain from Negative Talk

Negative comments can create a poor impression. Instead:

- **Stay Positive**: Focus on positive aspects of your experiences, avoiding gossip or complaints about others in the industry.
- **Support Others**: Celebrate the successes of others; it reflects well on you and fosters goodwill.

4. Don't Forget Cultural Sensitivities

In an increasingly globalized world, understanding cultural differences is vital. Be mindful of:

- **Different Communication Styles**: Be aware that some cultures may prefer direct communication while others value a more indirect approach.
- **Cultural Norms**: Research and understand basic cultural norms before attending networking events in diverse settings. Simple gestures, like a handshake or bow, can vary in significance.

Navigating Cultural Differences in Networking

1. Research and Understand

Before attending events with diverse attendees:

- **Learn About Cultural Practices**: Familiarize yourself with common cultural practices and norms that might affect communication styles.
- **Ask Questions**: If you're unsure about a cultural practice, don't hesitate to ask respectful questions.

2. Adapt Your Communication Style

Be flexible in your approach based on the cultural context:

- **Use Formality When Necessary**: Some cultures appreciate formal titles and language; adjust your tone accordingly.
- **Be Mindful of Nonverbal Cues**: Different cultures have varying interpretations of body language and gestures. Pay attention to these cues to avoid misunderstandings.

3. Be Patient and Open-Minded

Building relationships across cultures may require patience:

- **Take Time to Build Trust**: Recognize that some cultures prioritize building trust before diving into business discussions.
- **Stay Open to Learning**: Embrace cultural differences and view them as learning opportunities rather than obstacles.

Conclusion

Networking etiquette is essential for creating meaningful and lasting connections. By adhering to the dos and don'ts outlined in this chapter and being mindful of cultural differences, you can enhance your networking skills and increase your chances of success. As you continue to cultivate your network, remember that each interaction is an opportunity to build relationships that can lead to personal and professional growth. In the next chapter, we will delve into the fundamentals of understanding net worth, laying the groundwork for financial literacy and wealth-building strategies.

Chapter 13: From Network to Net Worth — Translating Connections into Capital

For twelve chapters, we have explored the mechanics, psychology, and etiquette of building meaningful relationships. We have discussed how to identify opportunities, craft a personal brand, follow up with intention, and build a network that is both diverse and deep. Now it is time to answer the question that sits at the heart of this book: *How does a strong network actually translate into net worth?*

Net worth, in the context of this book, is not merely the dollar figure on a balance sheet. It is the total measurable value — financial, professional, intellectual, and social — that flows from who you know, how well you know them, and how consistently you show up in their lives. Chapter 13 is the bridge between relationship-building and wealth-building.

13.1 Redefining Net Worth

Traditional definitions of net worth focus on assets minus liabilities. But professionals who have mastered networking understand that their most valuable assets rarely appear on a spreadsheet:

- **Financial Net Worth** — Savings, investments, property, and income-generating assets.
- **Professional Net Worth** — Skills, credentials, reputation, and career capital.
- **Social Net Worth** — The strength, reach, and trust-level of your network.
- **Intellectual Net Worth** — Knowledge, insights, and access to information others do not have.

When these four categories reinforce one another, wealth compounds. A strong social net worth opens doors to professional opportunities; professional advancement increases financial net worth; financial security frees your time to invest in learning and deeper relationships. The cycle feeds itself.

13.2 The Conversion Principle

Networks do not automatically become wealth. They must be *converted*, and conversion requires three ingredients:

1. **Clarity of Value** — You must know what you bring to the table and what you are seeking in return.
2. **Consistency of Contact** — Opportunities flow toward those who stay top-of-mind.
3. **Courage to Ask** — Most people never monetize their network because they never make a direct ask.

The networker who masters these three ingredients stops thinking of connections as "contacts" and begins treating them as co-creators of value.

13.3 The Five Currencies of a Network

Every connection you hold can produce value in one or more of five currencies:

1. **Information** — Market intelligence, industry trends, early knowledge of openings.
2. **Introductions** — Warm handoffs to decision-makers and collaborators.
3. **Influence** — Advocacy, endorsements, and references in rooms you are not in.
4. **Investment** — Capital, resources, or time committed to your ventures.
5. **Insight** — Mentorship, feedback, and hard-won wisdom.

Catalog your relationships by the currencies each can offer — and, equally important, by the currencies you offer in return. Reciprocity is the exchange rate of the networking economy.

13.4 Calculating the ROI of a Relationship

You cannot improve what you do not measure. While relationships should never be reduced to transactions, thoughtful networkers periodically assess the return on their relational investments. Consider tracking:

- **Opportunities sourced** from each connection over the past year.
- **Revenue or compensation** directly or indirectly tied to specific relationships.
- **Time invested** in nurturing the connection.
- **Value provided** to the other party.

A simple quarterly review will reveal which relationships are flourishing, which have gone dormant, and which may need reinvestment.

13.5 Turning Social Capital into Financial Capital

There are several proven pathways by which networks translate into tangible wealth:

- **Career Acceleration** — Referrals remain the single most common source of new hires and promotions.
- **Deal Flow** — Entrepreneurs, investors, and freelancers source the majority of their best opportunities through warm introductions.
- **Partnership and Equity** — Co-founders, joint ventures, and advisory roles frequently emerge from trusted relationships.
- **Client Acquisition** — Word-of-mouth referrals carry higher conversion rates and lower acquisition costs than any paid channel.
- **Access to Private Markets** — Angel rounds, off-market real estate, and exclusive funds are almost always network-gated.

13.6 Protecting the Asset

Your network is an appreciating asset — but only if you maintain it. Guard it with these practices:

- **Honor confidentiality.** A single leaked confidence can undo a decade of trust.
- **Deliver on promises.** Underpromise and overdeliver, especially on small things.
- **Give before you get.** A network built purely on taking will deplete itself.
- **Stay visible without being noisy.** Share wins, insights, and gratitude regularly.

13.7 A Framework for the Next Twelve Months

To put the principles of this chapter into practice, commit to the following over the next year:

1. Map your top 50 relationships and identify the currencies each offers and receives.
2. Set three measurable net worth goals — one financial, one professional, one social.
3. Schedule monthly "value outreach" — contacting five people with something useful, no ask attached.
4. Make one courageous ask per quarter that directly advances a stated goal.
5. Review and recalibrate every ninety days.

Key Takeaways

- Net worth is the sum of financial, professional, social, and intellectual capital.
- Networks must be actively converted into wealth through clarity, consistency, and courage.
- Relationships trade in five currencies: information, introductions, influence, investment, and insight.
- Measure the ROI of your network with the same seriousness you apply to any other asset.
- The goal is not to extract value from people — it is to build a system in which value circulates, and everyone inside the network grows richer for being part of it.

When network and net worth become one integrated system, wealth stops being something you chase and becomes something that arrives, steadily and predictably, through the people whose lives you have chosen to enrich.

Part 4: Understanding Net Worth Chapter 13: Defining Net Worth Assets vs. liabilities: what counts? The importance of tracking your net worth. Chapter 14: Financial Literacy Fundamentals Basic financial concepts everyone should know.

Resources for improving financial literacy. Chapter 15: Creating a Budget and Savings Plan Steps to develop a personal budget. Strategies for saving effectively. Chapter 16: Investing Basics Overview of investment options (stocks, bonds, real estate). Risk assessment and portfolio diversification. Part 5: Increasing Your Net Worth Chapter 17: Income Streams Identifying and creating multiple income sources. Passive income strategies. Chapter 18: Leveraging Networking for Financial Gains How to turn connections into clients or business opportunities. Networking tactics for entrepreneurs. Chapter 19: Building a Personal Development Plan Setting goals for career advancement. Investing in skills and education. Chapter 20: Risk Management and Insurance Importance of protecting your assets. Types of insurance to consider. Part 6: Sustaining Success Chapter 21: Giving Back and Community Engagement The role of philanthropy in networking and net worth. Building a legacy through community involvement. Chapter 22: Adapting to Change Staying relevant in a changing economy. Networking in a digital age. Chapter 23: Continuous Learning and Growth Emphasizing lifelong learning. Resources for ongoing education. Chapter 24: Measuring Your Success Tools for assessing networking and financial growth. Adjusting strategies based on results.

ChatGPT said:

ChatGPT

Chapter 13: Defining Net Worth

In the journey toward mastering both networking and net worth, understanding what net worth truly means is essential. It's not just a number on a balance sheet; it encapsulates your financial health and your ability to achieve your personal and professional goals. In this chapter, we will define net worth, differentiate between assets and liabilities, and emphasize the importance of tracking your net worth over time.

What is Net Worth?

Net worth is a straightforward calculation that represents the difference between what you own (assets) and what you owe (liabilities). It provides a snapshot of your financial position at a given point in time, allowing you to assess your overall financial health.

The Formula for Net Worth

The basic formula for calculating net worth is:

Net Worth = Total Assets - Total Liabilities

Assets

- **Cash and Cash Equivalents**: Savings accounts, cash on hand, and money market accounts.
- **Investments**: Stocks, bonds, mutual funds, retirement accounts (e.g., 401(k), IRA).
- **Real Estate**: The market value of your home and other properties.
- **Personal Property**: Valuable items such as cars, jewelry, and collectibles.

Liabilities

- **Mortgages**: Loans taken out to purchase real estate.
- **Student Loans**: Debts incurred for educational expenses.
- **Credit Card Debt**: Outstanding balances on credit cards.
- **Other Loans**: Personal loans, auto loans, or any other debt obligations.

What Counts as Assets?

When calculating your net worth, it's crucial to include all assets that can be easily converted to cash or have value. Here are some examples:

- **Liquid Assets**: Cash and cash equivalents are the easiest to liquidate and should be the first to consider.
- **Investments**: Stocks and bonds can fluctuate in value but represent potential future gains.
- **Real Estate**: Your home and any investment properties contribute significantly to your net worth, though it's important to assess their market value accurately.
- **Retirement Accounts**: These funds, although not immediately accessible without penalties, represent a significant portion of your future financial security.

What Counts as Liabilities?

Liabilities can detract from your net worth and represent the money you owe. They include:

- **Long-term Debts**: Mortgages and other loans that require years to pay off.
- **Short-term Debts**: Credit card balances and personal loans that need to be settled promptly.
- **Obligations**: Any financial commitments, such as alimony or child support.

The Importance of Tracking Your Net Worth

Understanding and regularly tracking your net worth can provide several benefits:

1. Measuring Financial Progress

Calculating your net worth periodically allows you to see how your financial situation evolves over time. This can motivate you to make smarter financial decisions, pay down debt, or increase savings.

2. Setting Financial Goals

Your net worth serves as a baseline for setting realistic financial goals. Whether you aim to increase savings, invest more, or purchase property, having a clear picture of your financial health helps you plan effectively.

3. Assessing Financial Health

Tracking your net worth can reveal patterns in your spending, saving, and investing habits. If your net worth is consistently declining, it might indicate that you need to reassess your financial strategies.

4. Planning for the Future

Knowing your net worth can help you prepare for significant life events, such as retirement, buying a home, or starting a business. It provides a framework for making informed decisions that align with your long-term objectives.

How to Calculate and Track Your Net Worth
Step 1: List Your Assets

Create a comprehensive list of all your assets and assign a value to each. Use recent market values or appraisals for real estate and personal property.

Step 2: List Your Liabilities

Detail all your debts and obligations, including outstanding balances and due dates. This ensures that you have an accurate picture of your financial commitments.

Step 3: Calculate Your Net Worth

Using the formula above, subtract your total liabilities from your total assets. This will give you your net worth.

Step 4: Monitor Regularly

Set a schedule to recalculate your net worth—quarterly or annually works well for many. This will help you track progress and make adjustments to your financial strategy.

Conclusion

Defining and tracking your net worth is a crucial aspect of mastering your financial health. By understanding the difference between assets and liabilities and regularly assessing your financial situation, you can make informed decisions that align with your goals. In the next chapter, we will explore financial literacy fundamentals, equipping you with the knowledge necessary to navigate your financial landscape confidently.

4o mini

You said:

Chapter 14: Measuring Your Networking Success and Net Worth Growth

Networking, like any worthwhile endeavor, requires measurement to understand its true impact. Without clear metrics, it's easy to mistake activity for progress—collecting business cards, attending events, and accumulating LinkedIn connections without actually advancing your personal or professional goals. This chapter provides a framework for evaluating the effectiveness of your networking efforts and connecting them directly to the growth of your net worth, both financial and relational.

The Relationship Between Network and Net Worth

It's often said that your network is your net worth. While this phrase has become something of a cliché, the underlying truth is profound: the people you know, the quality of your relationships, and your ability to mobilize them directly influence your opportunities, income, knowledge, and overall life satisfaction. Net worth, in its truest sense, extends beyond dollars and cents. It encompasses:

- **Financial capital**: Income, investments, assets, and earnings potential.
- **Social capital**: The value embedded in your relationships and connections.
- **Intellectual capital**: Knowledge, skills, and insights gained through others.
- **Reputational capital**: Your credibility, influence, and personal brand.
- **Emotional capital**: Support systems, mentorship, and friendships that sustain you.

A thriving network fuels growth across all five categories. Measuring your networking success, then, requires looking at each of these dimensions.

Key Performance Indicators for Networking

To accurately gauge your progress, consider tracking the following KPIs:

1. **Quality of Connections**: Rather than counting contacts, assess how many of your relationships are meaningful. Do you have people you can call for honest feedback, opportunities, or introductions?

2. **Opportunity Flow**: Track the number of opportunities—job offers, partnerships, speaking engagements, investment deals—that arrive through your network over a six- or twelve-month period.

3. **Referrals Given and Received**: A healthy network involves reciprocity. Measure how often you're introduced to new people and how often you're making introductions for others.

4. **Knowledge Acquisition**: Note the insights, lessons, and new skills you've gained through conversations, mentorships, and collaborative efforts.

5. **Income Influenced by Network**: Estimate the percentage of your earnings that can be traced back to a network contact—whether through referrals, clients, partnerships, or career moves.

6. **Response Rates**: How quickly and warmly do people respond to your outreach? This is a strong indicator of relational health.

Creating a Networking Scorecard

A simple scorecard can help you monitor progress. Divide your scorecard into monthly, quarterly, and annual columns, and include the following categories:

- New meaningful connections made
- Follow-ups completed
- Value provided to others (introductions, resources, support)
- Opportunities explored
- Mentors engaged
- Events attended
- Revenue or opportunities directly attributed to networking

Review this scorecard regularly. Patterns will emerge, revealing which activities yield the greatest return and which should be deprioritized.

Connecting Networking to Net Worth Growth

To tie your networking directly to net worth growth, adopt these strategies:

- **Audit your current network quarterly.** Identify relationships that energize and elevate you, and invest more deeply in them. Let dormant or draining connections fade naturally.
- **Align networking activities with financial goals.** If you're seeking a promotion, targeted networking with decision-makers matters more than attending generic mixers. If you're launching a business, connections with potential clients, investors, and partners take precedence.
- **Invest in high-leverage relationships.** A single well-placed mentor or strategic partner can accelerate your net worth more than hundreds of casual acquaintances.
- **Track financial outcomes.** Whenever a deal closes, a client signs, or a new role begins, note the origin. Over time, you'll see clearly which networking channels drive the most value.

Avoiding Vanity Metrics

Beware the trap of vanity metrics—numbers that look impressive but don't translate into meaningful outcomes. A LinkedIn following of 10,000 means little if none of those connections will return your calls. Likewise, attending fifty events a year is wasted effort if no substantive relationships result. Focus on depth and outcomes, not surface-level statistics.

Refining Your Strategy Over Time

Networking is not a static discipline. As your goals evolve, so too should your approach. Annually, set aside time to review your networking strategy:

- What worked well this year?
- Which relationships delivered the most value—and which did I contribute most to?
- Where did I fall short in follow-up or engagement?
- What new communities, industries, or demographics should I explore next year?
- How has my net worth—across all five forms of capital—grown?

By treating networking as a measurable, iterative practice, you transform it from a vague social activity into a disciplined engine of personal and professional growth.

Final Thoughts

Mastering the relationship between your network and your net worth requires intention, reflection, and consistent measurement. The people you surround yourself with shape the opportunities you see, the decisions you make, and the person you become. When you measure what matters, refine what doesn't, and invest in what works, your network becomes not just a collection of contacts but a compounding asset—one that grows in value year after year, enriching every dimension of your life.

Part 4: Understanding Net Worth Chapter 13: Defining Net Worth Assets vs. liabilities: what counts? The importance of tracking your net worth. Chapter 14: Financial Literacy Fundamentals Basic financial concepts everyone should know.

Resources for improving financial literacy. Chapter 15: Creating a Budget and Savings Plan Steps to develop a personal budget. Strategies for saving effectively. Chapter 16: Investing Basics Overview of investment options (stocks, bonds, real estate). Risk assessment and portfolio diversification. Part 5: Increasing Your Net Worth Chapter 17: Income Streams Identifying and creating multiple income sources. Passive income strategies. Chapter 18: Leveraging Networking for Financial Gains How to turn connections into clients or business opportunities. Networking tactics for entrepreneurs. Chapter 19: Building a Personal Development Plan Setting goals for career advancement. Investing in skills and education. Chapter 20: Risk Management and Insurance Importance of protecting your assets. Types of insurance to consider. Part 6: Sustaining Success Chapter 21: Giving Back and Community Engagement The role of philanthropy in networking and net worth. Building a legacy through community involvement. Chapter 22: Adapting to Change Staying relevant in a changing economy. Networking in a digital age. Chapter 23: Continuous Learning and Growth Emphasizing lifelong learning. Resources for ongoing education. Chapter 24: Measuring Your Success Tools for assessing networking and financial growth. Adjusting strategies based on results.

ChatGPT said:

ChatGPT

Chapter 14: Financial Literacy Fundamentals

Financial literacy is a critical skill set that empowers individuals to make informed financial decisions, manage their resources wisely, and achieve their personal and professional goals. In this chapter, we will explore the basic financial concepts everyone should understand, the significance of financial literacy, and resources available for improving your financial knowledge.

What is Financial Literacy?

Financial literacy is the ability to understand and effectively use various financial skills, including personal finance, budgeting, investing, and understanding financial products. It involves having the knowledge and confidence to make informed decisions about your money.

Why is Financial Literacy Important?

1. **Empowerment**: Financial literacy empowers individuals to take control of their finances, enabling them to make better decisions regarding spending, saving, and investing.
2. **Prevention of Debt**: Understanding financial principles helps individuals avoid falling into debt traps and manage existing debts more effectively.
3. **Improved Financial Security**: A strong grasp of financial concepts leads to better budgeting, saving for emergencies, and planning for retirement, ultimately enhancing financial security.
4. **Informed Investment Choices**: Knowledge of investing helps individuals grow their wealth and make educated choices about where to allocate their money.
5. **Building Wealth**: Financial literacy is foundational for building and sustaining wealth, enabling individuals to maximize their income and make their money work for them.

Basic Financial Concepts Everyone Should Know

1. Budgeting

Budgeting is the process of creating a plan for how to spend your money. A budget helps you allocate your income toward expenses, savings, and investments, ensuring you live within your means. Key components include:

- **Income**: Total earnings from all sources (salary, side jobs, investments).
- **Expenses**: Fixed (rent, utilities) and variable (entertainment, groceries) costs.
- **Savings**: Setting aside money for emergencies, retirement, and future goals.

2. Saving

Saving is the practice of setting aside a portion of your income for future use. It's essential for achieving financial stability and preparing for unexpected expenses. Consider these saving strategies:

- **Emergency Fund**: Aim to save three to six months' worth of living expenses in a separate account for unforeseen emergencies.
- **Savings Goals**: Set specific goals for short-term (vacations, purchases) and long-term (home down payment, retirement) savings.

3. Credit Management

Credit management involves understanding how credit works, maintaining a good credit score, and managing debt responsibly. Key elements include:

- **Credit Score**: A numerical representation of your creditworthiness, influencing your ability to borrow money and the interest rates you receive.
- **Debt-to-Income Ratio**: A measure of how much of your income goes toward paying debts, impacting your credit applications.
- **Responsible Borrowing**: Use credit cards and loans wisely, ensuring you can repay what you borrow without accruing excessive interest or fees.

4. Understanding Interest Rates

Interest rates determine how much you pay to borrow money or earn on your savings. Familiarize yourself with:

- **APY (Annual Percentage Yield)**: The rate of return on your savings account, reflecting the interest earned annually.
- **APR (Annual Percentage Rate)**: The cost of borrowing expressed as a yearly interest rate. A lower APR is preferable when taking out loans or using credit cards.

5. Investing Basics

Investing is putting your money to work in assets that have the potential to grow in value. Key concepts include:

- **Types of Investments**: Stocks, bonds, mutual funds, real estate, and alternative investments.
- **Risk vs. Reward**: Higher potential returns often come with higher risk. Understanding your risk tolerance is crucial for successful investing.
- **Diversification**: Spreading your investments across different asset classes to mitigate risk.

6. Retirement Planning

Planning for retirement involves setting aside funds to ensure financial stability in your later years. Consider:

- **Retirement Accounts**: Familiarize yourself with 401(k)s, IRAs, and other retirement savings options, including their tax advantages.
- **Contribution Strategies**: Aim to contribute regularly, taking advantage of employer matches and increasing contributions as income rises.

Resources for Improving Financial Literacy

1. **Books**: Explore titles such as *The Total Money Makeover* by Dave Ramsey and *Rich Dad Poor Dad* by Robert Kiyosaki, which offer foundational financial principles.
2. **Online Courses**: Websites like Coursera, Udemy, and Khan Academy provide financial literacy courses that cover various topics from budgeting to investing.
3. **Podcasts and Blogs**: Follow financial experts who share insights, tips, and strategies on managing money. Popular options include *The Dave Ramsey Show* and *The Money Girl Podcast*.
4. **Financial Advisors**: Consider working with a certified financial planner to receive personalized advice tailored to your financial situation and goals.
5. **Local Workshops**: Many community organizations and financial institutions offer free or low-cost workshops on budgeting, investing, and credit management.

Conclusion

Financial literacy is an essential skill that enhances your ability to manage your personal finances, make informed decisions, and work toward your goals. By mastering the fundamental concepts of budgeting, saving, credit management, investing, and retirement planning, you can set a strong foundation for your financial future. In the next chapter, we will explore practical steps for creating a budget and savings plan that aligns with your financial aspirations.

4o mini

You said:

write chapter 15 for the book Mastering Network and Net Worth Chapter 1: Understanding Networking Definition and significance of networking. Different types of networks (personal, professional, social). Chapter 2: The Psychology of Networking Building trust and rapport. Overcoming networking anxiety. Chapter 3: Identifying Your Networking Goals Assessing personal and professional aspirations. Setting measurable networking objectives. Chapter 4: Building Your Personal Brand Crafting your personal story. Importance of online presence (LinkedIn, social media). Part 2: Expanding Your Network Chapter 5: Where to Network Identifying key networking opportunities (conferences, seminars, online platforms). Leveraging community events and local groups. Chapter 6: The Art of Conversation Effective communication skills. Active listening and engagement techniques. Chapter 7: Follow-Up Strategies Importance of timely follow-ups. Best practices for staying connected. Chapter 8: Building a Diverse Network Benefits of diversity in connections. Strategies for reaching out to different demographics. Part 3: Leveraging Your Network for Success Chapter 9: Networking for Opportunities How to identify and seize opportunities through connections. Case studies of successful networking. Chapter 10: Mentorship and Guidance Finding and nurturing mentor-mentee relationships. The role of mentorship in personal growth. Chapter 11: Collaborative Networking Building partnerships for mutual benefit. Examples of successful collaborations. Chapter 12: Networking Etiquette Dos and don'ts of professional networking. Navigating cultural differences in networking.

Part 4: Understanding Net Worth Chapter 13: Defining Net Worth Assets vs. liabilities: what counts? The importance of tracking your net worth. Chapter 14: Financial Literacy Fundamentals Basic financial concepts everyone should know.

Resources for improving financial literacy. Chapter 15: Creating a Budget and Savings Plan Steps to develop a personal budget. Strategies for saving effectively. Chapter 16: Investing Basics Overview of investment options (stocks, bonds, real estate). Risk assessment and portfolio diversification. Part 5: Increasing Your Net Worth Chapter 17: Income Streams Identifying and creating multiple income sources. Passive income strategies. Chapter 18: Leveraging Networking for Financial Gains How to turn connections into clients or business opportunities. Networking tactics for entrepreneurs. Chapter 19: Building a Personal Development Plan Setting goals for career advancement. Investing in skills and education. Chapter 20: Risk Management and Insurance Importance of protecting your assets. Types of insurance to consider. Part 6: Sustaining Success Chapter 21: Giving Back and Community Engagement The role of philanthropy in networking and net worth. Building a legacy through community involvement. Chapter 22: Adapting to Change Staying relevant in a changing economy. Networking in a digital age. Chapter 23: Continuous Learning and Growth Emphasizing lifelong learning. Resources for ongoing education. Chapter 24: Measuring Your Success Tools for assessing networking and financial growth. Adjusting strategies based on results.

ChatGPT said:

ChatGPT

Chapter 15: Creating a Budget and Savings Plan

Creating a budget and savings plan is crucial for managing your finances effectively and achieving your financial goals. In this chapter, we will outline the steps for developing a comprehensive personal budget and discuss strategies for saving effectively.

The Importance of Budgeting

A budget serves as a financial roadmap, helping you understand where your money goes, control your spending, and allocate funds for savings and investments. Key benefits of budgeting include:

1. **Enhanced Financial Awareness**: A budget provides clarity on your income and expenses, allowing you to identify spending patterns and areas for improvement.
2. **Goal Achievement**: By allocating funds toward specific goals (e.g., emergency fund, vacation, retirement), a budget helps you prioritize and stay focused.
3. **Debt Management**: A well-structured budget can aid in managing and reducing debt by ensuring you have funds available for regular payments.
4. **Peace of Mind**: Knowing you have a plan for your finances can reduce anxiety and increase confidence in your financial decision-making.

Steps to Develop a Personal Budget

1. Assess Your Income

Start by calculating your total monthly income. Include all sources of income, such as:

- Salary or wages
- Bonuses or commissions
- Freelance work or side jobs
- Investment income (dividends, interest)
- Any other sources of regular income

2. Track Your Expenses

Next, track your expenses to understand where your money is going. Categorize your expenses into fixed and variable:

- **Fixed Expenses**: These are consistent costs that do not change month to month, such as rent/mortgage, insurance premiums, and loan payments.
- **Variable Expenses**: These fluctuate based on usage or personal choices, including groceries, dining out, entertainment, and clothing.

Keep track of your expenses for at least a month to get an accurate picture of your spending habits. You can use budgeting apps, spreadsheets, or pen and paper—whatever works best for you.

3. Create Spending Categories

After tracking your expenses, create categories to group similar items together. Common categories include:

- Housing (rent/mortgage, utilities)
- Transportation (gas, public transport, car payments)
- Food (groceries, dining out)
- Health (medical expenses, insurance)
- Entertainment (movies, hobbies)
- Savings and Investments (retirement contributions, emergency fund)

4. Set Your Budget

With your income and expenses categorized, it's time to set your budget. Allocate a specific amount to each category based on your financial goals and priorities. Make sure to:

- **Prioritize Needs Over Wants**: Ensure your basic needs (housing, food, transportation) are covered before allocating funds for discretionary spending.
- **Include Savings**: Treat savings as a non-negotiable expense by allocating a portion of your income to savings before anything else.

5. Review and Adjust Regularly

Your budget should be a living document that adapts to changes in your life and financial situation. Schedule regular reviews (monthly or quarterly) to assess your budget's effectiveness and make adjustments as needed. Consider the following:

- Are you staying within your budget?
- Are there areas where you can cut back on spending?
- Have your financial goals changed?

Strategies for Saving Effectively

1. Set Clear Savings Goals

Identify specific savings goals, both short-term (vacation, emergency fund) and long-term (home purchase, retirement). Having clear goals will motivate you to save consistently.

2. Pay Yourself First

Treat savings as a mandatory expense. Set up automatic transfers from your checking account to a savings account each month, ensuring that you prioritize saving before spending.

3. Establish an Emergency Fund

Aim to save three to six months' worth of living expenses in a separate account to cover unexpected expenses (medical emergencies, job loss, urgent home repairs). This fund provides financial security and peace of mind.

4. Cut Unnecessary Expenses

Review your spending habits to identify areas where you can cut back. Consider these strategies:

- Limit dining out and cook at home more often.
- Cancel unused subscriptions or memberships.
- Look for discounts and coupons when shopping.

5. Use High-Interest Savings Accounts

Choose a high-yield savings account to earn more interest on your savings. This will help your money grow while remaining accessible for emergencies or future goals.

6. Take Advantage of Employer-Sponsored Savings Programs

If your employer offers a retirement savings plan (like a 401(k)) with matching contributions, take full advantage of it. Contribute at least enough to get the full match, as this is essentially "free money."

7. Regularly Reevaluate Your Goals and Progress

Periodically assess your savings goals and progress toward achieving them. Celebrate small milestones and adjust your plan if necessary to stay on track.

Conclusion

Creating a budget and savings plan is an essential step toward achieving financial stability and reaching your financial goals. By understanding your income and expenses, setting clear goals, and implementing effective saving strategies, you can take control of your finances and pave the way for a secure financial future. In the next chapter, we will explore the basics of investing and how to grow your wealth through informed investment choices.

4o mini

You said:

Chapter 16: Sustaining Your Network for Long-Term Net Worth

Networking is not a sprint—it is a lifelong marathon. While previous chapters have shown you how to build, expand, and leverage your connections, this chapter focuses on the often-overlooked discipline of *sustaining* your network so that it continues to compound in value, much like a well-managed financial portfolio. The true measure of a network's worth is not its size at any single moment, but its durability, depth, and relevance over decades.

The Compounding Effect of Relationships

Just as money invested wisely grows through compound interest, relationships nurtured consistently grow in trust, influence, and opportunity. A connection made today may seem insignificant, but ten years from now, that same person could become a client, a business partner, a mentor, or the gateway to an opportunity you never imagined. Sustaining your network means recognizing that every interaction is a deposit into a long-term relational account.

Key principles of relational compounding:

- **Consistency over intensity.** A brief, thoughtful message every few months outperforms a flurry of contact followed by years of silence.
- **Give before you get.** Offer value—introductions, insights, encouragement—without expecting immediate return.
- **Stay visible.** Share your wins, lessons, and milestones so your network remembers who you are and what you do.

Auditing Your Network Regularly

A sustainable network requires periodic review. At least once a year, conduct a "relationship audit":

1. **List your key contacts.** Identify the 50–100 people who matter most to your personal and professional life.
2. **Assess relationship health.** When did you last speak? Is the connection warm, lukewarm, or dormant?
3. **Categorize by purpose.** Mentors, peers, collaborators, clients, advocates, and friends each play different roles.
4. **Identify gaps.** Are you missing voices in certain industries, generations, or geographies?
5. **Plan re-engagement.** Schedule outreach to revive dormant but valuable ties.

This audit is not transactional—it is stewardship. You are tending a garden, not managing a spreadsheet.

Systems for Staying Connected

Sustaining a network of hundreds of people requires systems, not willpower. Consider:

- **A contact management system (CRM).** Tools like Notion, Airtable, HubSpot, or even a simple spreadsheet can track names, conversations, birthdays, interests, and follow-up dates.
- **The "five-a-day" rule.** Reach out to five people each day—a quick text, a comment on their post, a shared article. In a year, that's over 1,800 touchpoints.
- **Monthly "catch-up" blocks.** Dedicate specific hours each month for calls with long-term contacts.
- **Annual rituals.** Holiday cards, birthday notes, or a personal year-in-review email keep you top of mind.

Evolving With Your Network

People change, and so must your relationships. The college friend who once shared your ambitions may now lead a company. The junior colleague you mentored may become the executive who hires you. Sustaining your network means honoring these transformations—celebrating promotions, acknowledging setbacks, and adjusting your approach as roles shift.

Be willing to:

- **Reintroduce yourself.** As your career evolves, remind contacts who you are now, not who you were.
- **Let some connections fade gracefully.** Not every relationship is meant to last forever, and that's okay.
- **Invest in new generations.** Bring younger professionals into your orbit; they will shape the future of your network.

Turning Network Into Net Worth

Net worth is not merely financial—it is the sum of the resources, relationships, knowledge, and influence you can call upon. A sustained network translates into:

- **Career resilience.** When industries shift or jobs disappear, your network becomes your safety net.
- **Business growth.** Repeat clients, referrals, and partnerships emerge from long-standing trust.
- **Personal fulfillment.** Deep connections enrich life in ways money cannot.
- **Legacy.** The people you uplift become part of your enduring impact.

Practical Exercise: The Ten-Year Vision

Imagine your network ten years from now. Who do you want to still be connected with? Who do you hope to have added? What reputation do you want to carry among them? Write this vision down, then reverse-engineer the habits, rituals, and investments needed to make it real.

Chapter Summary

Sustaining your network is the bridge between short-term connection and long-term net worth. It requires consistency, systems, generosity, and evolution. Those who master this discipline discover that their network becomes their greatest compounding asset—one that pays dividends in opportunity, wisdom, and wealth for the rest of their lives.

Reflection Questions:

1. Which five relationships in your network have compounded the most value over time, and why?
2. What system will you implement this month to stay consistently connected?
3. Who in your network deserves re-engagement after too long a silence?
4. How will you measure the health of your network one year from today?

Part 4: Understanding Net Worth

Chapter 13: Defining Net Worth
Assets vs. liabilities: what counts? The importance of tracking your net worth.

Chapter 14: Financial Literacy Fundamentals
Basic financial concepts everyone should know. Resources for improving financial literacy.

Chapter 15: Creating a Budget and Savings Plan
Steps to develop a personal budget. Strategies for saving effectively.

Chapter 16: Investing Basics
Overview of investment options (stocks, bonds, real estate). Risk assessment and portfolio diversification.

Part 5: Increasing Your Net Worth

Chapter 17: Income Streams
Identifying and creating multiple income sources. Passive income strategies.

Chapter 18: Leveraging Networking for Financial Gains
How to turn connections into clients or business opportunities. Networking tactics for entrepreneurs.

Chapter 19: Building a Personal Development Plan
Setting goals for career advancement. Investing in skills and education.

Chapter 20: Risk Management and Insurance
Importance of protecting your assets. Types of insurance to consider.

Part 6: Sustaining Success

Chapter 21: Giving Back and Community Engagement
The role of philanthropy in networking and net worth. Building a legacy through community involvement.

Chapter 22: Adapting to Change
Staying relevant in a changing economy. Networking in a digital age.

Chapter 23: Continuous Learning and Growth
Emphasizing lifelong learning. Resources for ongoing education.

Chapter 24: Measuring Your Success
Tools for assessing networking and financial growth. Adjusting strategies based on results.

ChatGPT said:

ChatGPT

Chapter 16: Investing Basics

Investing is a fundamental component of building wealth and increasing your net worth. It involves allocating resources, usually money, in order to generate income or profit over time. This chapter provides an overview of investment options, the importance of risk assessment, and strategies for portfolio diversification.

Understanding Investment Options

Investing can take many forms, and understanding the different types can help you make informed decisions based on your financial goals, risk tolerance, and time horizon. Here are some common investment options:

1. Stocks

Definition: Stocks represent ownership in a company. When you buy a share of stock, you become a part-owner of that company.

Potential Returns: Stocks have historically offered higher returns compared to other investments, but they come with higher risk.

Considerations: The stock market can be volatile, and individual stocks can fluctuate significantly in value. Diversifying your stock holdings across various sectors can mitigate some of this risk.

2. Bonds

Definition: Bonds are loans made to corporations or governments in exchange for periodic interest payments and the return of the bond's face value at maturity.

Potential Returns: Generally, bonds are considered safer than stocks, but they typically offer lower returns. They can provide a steady income stream and can act as a buffer against stock market volatility.

Considerations: Different types of bonds (government, municipal, corporate) have varying levels of risk and returns. Understanding the creditworthiness of the issuer is crucial.

3. Mutual Funds

Definition: Mutual funds pool money from multiple investors to invest in a diversified portfolio of stocks, bonds, or other securities.

Potential Returns: The return on mutual funds depends on the performance of the underlying assets. They can provide diversification and professional management.

Considerations: Mutual funds charge management fees, which can impact overall returns. It's essential to research fund performance and fees before investing.

4. Exchange-Traded Funds (ETFs)

Definition: ETFs are similar to mutual funds but trade on stock exchanges like individual stocks. They usually track an index and offer diversification across various assets.

Potential Returns: ETFs generally have lower fees compared to mutual funds and offer liquidity due to their trading nature.

Considerations: Like stocks, the price of ETFs fluctuates throughout the trading day, and investors should consider the underlying assets when investing.

5. Real Estate

Definition: Investing in real estate involves purchasing property for rental income or appreciation.

Potential Returns: Real estate can provide a steady income stream through rents and potential for significant appreciation over time.

Considerations: Real estate requires substantial capital, ongoing maintenance, and market knowledge. Consider investing in real estate investment trusts (REITs) for easier access to real estate markets.

6. Commodities

Definition: Commodities include physical goods like gold, silver, oil, and agricultural products. Investors can buy physical commodities or invest in commodity futures.

Potential Returns: Commodities can serve as a hedge against inflation and market volatility.

Considerations: Commodities can be highly volatile and influenced by global supply and demand factors. Proper research is essential before investing.

7. Cryptocurrencies

Definition: Cryptocurrencies are digital or virtual currencies that use cryptography for security. Bitcoin is the most well-known cryptocurrency.

Potential Returns: Cryptocurrencies have experienced exponential growth in recent years, offering high potential returns.

Considerations: The cryptocurrency market is highly speculative and volatile. Investors should be cautious and only invest what they can afford to lose.

Risk Assessment in Investing

Understanding risk is vital in the investment process. Every investment carries some level of risk, and your risk tolerance should dictate your investment choices. Here are key factors to consider when assessing risk:

1. Risk Tolerance

Your risk tolerance is your ability and willingness to endure fluctuations in your investment portfolio. Factors influencing your risk tolerance include:

- **Time Horizon**: Longer investment horizons generally allow for greater risk-taking, as there's more time to recover from market downturns.
- **Financial Situation**: Individuals with more disposable income may be more comfortable with higher-risk investments.
- **Investment Goals**: Understanding whether your goal is capital preservation, income generation, or aggressive growth can guide your investment strategy.

2. Market Risk

Market risk refers to the potential for an investment's value to decrease due to market fluctuations. This risk affects all types of investments, particularly stocks and ETFs.

3. Credit Risk

Credit risk is associated with bonds and refers to the possibility that the bond issuer may default on payments. Research the credit rating of bond issuers to assess this risk.

4. Inflation Risk

Inflation risk is the risk that rising prices will erode your investment returns. Investments that do not keep pace with inflation may lose purchasing power over time.

5. Diversification

Diversification involves spreading your investments across various asset classes and sectors to reduce overall risk. A diversified portfolio can withstand market fluctuations better than a concentrated one.

Portfolio Diversification

Building a diversified investment portfolio is key to managing risk and optimizing returns. Here are some strategies for diversification:

1. Asset Allocation

Asset allocation involves dividing your investment portfolio among different asset categories, such as stocks, bonds, and cash. A common strategy is to adjust your allocation based on your age and risk tolerance, typically holding more stocks when younger and gradually shifting to bonds as you near retirement.

2. Sector Diversification

Investing across different sectors (e.g., technology, healthcare, finance) helps mitigate the impact of sector-specific downturns.

3. Geographic Diversification

Consider investing in both domestic and international markets. Global investments can reduce exposure to economic downturns in any single country.

4. Rebalancing

Regularly reviewing and rebalancing your portfolio ensures that your asset allocation aligns with your investment goals and risk tolerance. This involves selling assets that have increased in value and buying those that have decreased, maintaining your desired asset mix.

Conclusion

Understanding the basics of investing is crucial for increasing your net worth and achieving long-term financial goals. By exploring various investment options, assessing risks, and diversifying your portfolio, you can build a solid foundation for wealth accumulation. In the next chapter, we will delve into the various income streams you can create to further enhance your financial growth.

4o mini

You said:

Chapter 17: Measuring and Evaluating Your Networking Success

In the journey of mastering network and net worth, it is essential not only to build and nurture your connections but also to measure and evaluate the success of your networking efforts. Without assessment, it becomes difficult to know whether your strategies are working, where to improve, and how to maximize the return on the time and energy you invest in relationships. This chapter explores the frameworks, metrics, and reflective practices that will help you gauge the effectiveness of your networking and refine your approach for continued growth.

The Importance of Measuring Networking Success

Networking is often viewed as an intangible activity — a series of conversations, handshakes, and follow-ups that may or may not lead to meaningful outcomes. However, like any other professional endeavor, networking can and should be measured. Measurement transforms networking from a vague effort into a strategic practice. It allows you to:

- Identify which relationships and activities generate the most value.
- Recognize gaps in your network that need attention.
- Justify the time and resources you dedicate to networking.
- Set benchmarks for future growth.
- Celebrate milestones and progress along the way.

Without measurement, networking can feel aimless. With it, you gain clarity, focus, and confidence in your approach.

Defining Success in Networking

Before you can measure success, you must define what success means to you. Networking success is deeply personal and varies depending on your goals. For some, success may mean landing a new job, closing a business deal, or securing a mentor. For others, it may involve building a community, gaining industry insights, or simply expanding one's circle of trusted peers.

To define success, revisit the goals you set in earlier chapters. Ask yourself:

- What outcomes did I hope to achieve through networking?
- Which relationships are most aligned with my aspirations?
- How do I want my network to support my personal and professional growth?

By clarifying your definition of success, you create a foundation for meaningful measurement.

Key Metrics for Evaluating Networking Success

While networking is relational, there are quantitative and qualitative metrics that can help you evaluate your progress. Consider the following:

1. **Network Growth**: Track the number of new, meaningful connections you add over time. Focus on quality rather than quantity — a handful of strong relationships often outweigh hundreds of superficial ones.

2. **Engagement Levels**: Measure how often you interact with your network. Are you regularly reaching out, following up, and engaging in meaningful conversations?

3. **Opportunities Generated**: Keep a record of the opportunities — job offers, collaborations, referrals, introductions — that come through your network.

4. **Reciprocity**: Evaluate the balance of give-and-take in your relationships. Are you offering value to others as much as you receive?

5. **Diversity of Network**: Assess the variety of industries, backgrounds, and perspectives represented in your network. A diverse network often yields richer opportunities.

6. **Personal Growth**: Reflect on how your network has contributed to your learning, skill development, and confidence.

Tools for Tracking Networking Progress

To measure networking effectively, you need systems in place. Some practical tools include:

- **CRM Software**: Platforms like HubSpot, Salesforce, or even simple spreadsheets can help you track contacts, interactions, and follow-ups.
- **LinkedIn Analytics**: Monitor profile views, connection requests, and engagement with your posts to gauge your online presence.
- **Journaling**: Keep a networking journal to record conversations, insights, and reflections after each interaction.
- **Goal-Tracking Apps**: Use apps like Trello, Notion, or Asana to set and track networking objectives.

These tools not only help you stay organized but also provide data to evaluate your progress.

Reflecting on Qualitative Outcomes

Not all networking success can be captured in numbers. Qualitative outcomes often reveal the deeper impact of your efforts. Reflect on questions such as:

- Have my relationships deepened over time?
- Am I learning from the people in my network?
- Do I feel supported and inspired by my connections?
- Have I been able to support others in meaningful ways?

These reflections provide a holistic view of your networking journey, reminding you that success is not just about transactions but about transformation.

Adjusting Your Strategy Based on Evaluation

Measurement is only valuable if it leads to action. Once you evaluate your networking success, use the insights to refine your approach. For example:

- If your network lacks diversity, seek out events or groups outside your usual circles.
- If engagement is low, commit to a consistent follow-up schedule.
- If opportunities are limited, focus on building deeper relationships with key connections.
- If reciprocity is unbalanced, find new ways to add value to others.

By continuously evaluating and adjusting, you ensure that your networking remains dynamic, purposeful, and aligned with your evolving goals.

Celebrating Milestones

Finally, remember to celebrate your networking milestones. Whether it's landing a dream mentor, building a thriving community, or simply overcoming networking anxiety, each step forward deserves recognition. Celebrating milestones reinforces positive habits, motivates continued growth, and reminds you of the value of your efforts.

Conclusion

Measuring and evaluating your networking success is a vital practice in mastering both your network and your net worth. By defining success, tracking key metrics, reflecting on qualitative outcomes, and adjusting your strategies, you transform networking into a deliberate and rewarding journey. Remember, networking is not a one-time achievement but an ongoing process of growth, connection, and contribution. With consistent evaluation, you can ensure that your network continues to thrive and serve as a powerful asset in your personal and professional life.

Part 4: Understanding Net Worth Chapter 13: Defining Net Worth Assets vs. liabilities: what counts? The importance of tracking your net worth. Chapter 14: Financial Literacy Fundamentals Basic financial concepts everyone should know.

Resources for improving financial literacy. Chapter 15: Creating a Budget and Savings Plan Steps to develop a personal budget. Strategies for saving effectively. Chapter 16: Investing Basics Overview of investment options (stocks, bonds, real estate). Risk assessment and portfolio diversification. Part 5: Increasing Your Net Worth Chapter 17: Income Streams Identifying and creating multiple income sources. Passive income strategies. Chapter 18: Leveraging Networking for Financial Gains How to turn connections into clients or business opportunities. Networking tactics for entrepreneurs. Chapter 19: Building a Personal Development Plan Setting goals for career advancement. Investing in skills and education. Chapter 20: Risk Management and Insurance Importance of protecting your assets. Types of insurance to consider. Part 6: Sustaining Success Chapter 21: Giving Back and Community Engagement The role of philanthropy in networking and net worth. Building a legacy through community involvement. Chapter 22: Adapting to Change Staying relevant in a changing economy. Networking in a digital age. Chapter 23: Continuous Learning and Growth Emphasizing lifelong learning. Resources for ongoing education. Chapter 24: Measuring Your Success Tools for assessing networking and financial growth. Adjusting strategies based on results.

ChatGPT said:

ChatGPT

Chapter 17: Income Streams

Creating and diversifying income streams is a crucial step in mastering your net worth. Relying on a single source of income can leave you vulnerable to financial instability. This chapter explores various types of income streams, emphasizing both active and passive options, and provides strategies for effectively implementing them.

Understanding Income Streams

An **income stream** is a source from which you receive money. Income streams can be classified into two main categories: active income and passive income.

Active Income

Active income refers to earnings that require continuous effort or work to sustain. Common examples include:

1. **Salary and Wages**: The most common form of active income is earned from a job or self-employment. This requires consistent work hours in exchange for compensation.
2. **Freelancing**: Offering your skills and services on a project basis. Freelancers can work in various fields, including writing, graphic design, consulting, and more.
3. **Consulting**: Leveraging your expertise to provide advice and guidance to businesses or individuals on a contractual basis.
4. **Teaching or Tutoring**: Sharing your knowledge or skills through formal or informal education, either online or in person.

Passive Income

Passive income, on the other hand, requires less ongoing effort and can provide financial rewards with minimal active participation. It's an essential component of wealth-building strategies. Here are some common forms of passive income:

1. **Real Estate Investments**: Owning rental properties can generate monthly income while appreciating over time. Alternatively, investing in real estate investment trusts (REITs) allows you to earn passive income without direct property management.
2. **Dividend Stocks**: Investing in stocks that pay dividends provides a regular income stream. Dividend-paying companies distribute a portion of their earnings to shareholders, typically on a quarterly basis.
3. **Interest from Savings Accounts or Bonds**: Savings accounts and bonds can yield interest payments, contributing to your passive income.
4. **Royalties**: If you create intellectual property—like books, music, or patents—you can earn royalties when others use or sell your creations.
5. **Online Courses or E-books**: Creating and selling educational content can provide ongoing revenue. Once developed, these products can generate income with little additional effort.
6. **Affiliate Marketing**: Promoting other companies' products or services online and earning a commission for every sale made through your referral link.

Identifying Your Income Streams

Identifying the right income streams for you requires assessing your skills, resources, interests, and risk tolerance. Here are steps to help you pinpoint the best options:

1. **Evaluate Your Skills and Interests**: Identify what you are good at and what you enjoy doing. This can guide your decision on which income streams to pursue.
2. **Research Opportunities**: Investigate various income sources available in your field of expertise. Stay informed about trends and demands in the marketplace.
3. **Consider Your Financial Situation**: Assess your current financial position and how much time and capital you can invest in creating new income streams.
4. **Diversification**: Aim for a mix of both active and passive income streams to create a balanced financial portfolio. This approach can help stabilize your income, especially in uncertain economic times.

Strategies for Creating Multiple Income Streams

Once you have identified potential income streams, the next step is to implement strategies to create and grow them effectively.

1. Start Small and Scale Up

Begin with one or two income streams that require less initial investment or effort. As you gain experience and confidence, gradually expand your portfolio. For instance, start freelancing in your spare time while maintaining your full-time job.

2. Automate Where Possible

For passive income streams, look for opportunities to automate processes. Use technology to manage investments, online sales, and marketing efforts. For example, consider using e-commerce platforms that automate payment processing and customer management.

3. Leverage Your Network

Utilize your networking skills to identify opportunities for collaboration and partnership. Engaging with others in your industry can lead to new income opportunities, referrals, and mentorship.

4. Continuous Learning

Stay informed about new trends and skills relevant to your income streams. Invest in education or training to enhance your knowledge and capabilities, which can lead to higher income potential.

5. Reinvest Earnings

Consider reinvesting a portion of your passive income into your income-generating activities. For instance, use dividends or rental income to acquire more stocks or properties, thus compounding your earnings.

6. Monitor and Adjust

Regularly review your income streams to assess their performance. Track which sources are thriving and which may require adjustment or replacement. This helps in optimizing your income strategy and maximizing returns.

Conclusion

Building multiple income streams is essential for increasing your net worth and achieving financial stability. By diversifying your income sources, you not only enhance your earnings potential but also reduce your financial risks. In the next chapter, we will explore how to leverage your network for financial gains, turning connections into valuable business opportunities.

write chapter 18 for the book Mastering Network and Net Worth Chapter 1: Understanding Networking Definition and significance of networking. Different types of networks (personal, professional, social). Chapter 2: The Psychology of Networking Building trust and rapport. Overcoming networking anxiety. Chapter 3: Identifying Your Networking Goals Assessing personal and professional aspirations. Setting measurable networking objectives. Chapter 4: Building Your Personal Brand Crafting your personal story. Importance of online presence (LinkedIn, social media). Part 2: Expanding Your Network Chapter 5: Where to Network Identifying key networking opportunities (conferences, seminars, online platforms). Leveraging community events and local groups. Chapter 6: The Art of Conversation Effective communication skills. Active listening and engagement techniques. Chapter 7: Follow-Up Strategies Importance of timely follow-ups. Best practices for staying connected. Chapter 8: Building a Diverse Network Benefits of diversity in connections. Strategies for reaching out to different demographics. Part 3: Leveraging Your Network for Success Chapter 9: Networking for Opportunities How to identify and seize opportunities through connections. Case studies of successful networking. Chapter 10: Mentorship and Guidance Finding and nurturing mentor-mentee relationships. The role of mentorship in personal growth. Chapter 11: Collaborative Networking Building partnerships for mutual benefit. Examples of successful collaborations. Chapter 12: Networking Etiquette Dos and don'ts of professional networking. Navigating cultural differences in networking.

Part 4: Understanding Net Worth

Chapter 13: Defining Net Worth
Assets vs. liabilities: what counts?
The importance of tracking your net worth.

Chapter 14: Financial Literacy Fundamentals
Basic financial concepts everyone should know.
Resources for improving financial literacy.

Chapter 15: Creating a Budget and Savings Plan
Steps to develop a personal budget.
Strategies for saving effectively.

Chapter 16: Investing Basics
Overview of investment options (stocks, bonds, real estate).
Risk assessment and portfolio diversification.

Part 5: Increasing Your Net Worth

Chapter 17: Income Streams
Identifying and creating multiple income sources.
Passive income strategies.

Chapter 18: Leveraging Networking for Financial Gains
How to turn connections into clients or business opportunities.
Networking tactics for entrepreneurs.

Chapter 19: Building a Personal Development Plan
Setting goals for career advancement.
Investing in skills and education.

Chapter 20: Risk Management and Insurance
Importance of protecting your assets.
Types of insurance to consider.

Part 6: Sustaining Success

Chapter 21: Giving Back and Community Engagement
The role of philanthropy in networking and net worth.
Building a legacy through community involvement.

Chapter 22: Adapting to Change
Staying relevant in a changing economy.
Networking in a digital age.

Chapter 23: Continuous Learning and Growth
Emphasizing lifelong learning.
Resources for ongoing education.

Chapter 24: Measuring Your Success
Tools for assessing networking and financial growth.
Adjusting strategies based on results.

ChatGPT said:

ChatGPT

Chapter 18: Leveraging Networking for Financial Gains

In today's interconnected world, networking is not just about making connections; it's about harnessing those relationships to create financial opportunities. This chapter explores how to effectively leverage your network to turn connections into clients or business opportunities, providing actionable strategies for entrepreneurs and professionals alike.

Understanding the Value of Your Network

Your network is a powerful asset. Each connection you make can open doors to opportunities that can significantly enhance your financial position. Recognizing the potential within your network is the first step toward leveraging it for financial gains. Here are key components of this value:

1. **Access to Resources**: Your connections can provide valuable resources, including knowledge, advice, and tools that can help you advance in your career or business.
2. **Opportunities for Collaboration**: Collaborating with others in your network can lead to new projects, partnerships, or ventures that can generate income.
3. **Referrals and Recommendations**: Personal recommendations from trusted contacts can lead to new clients or business opportunities, as people are more likely to engage with someone who comes highly recommended.
4. **Market Insights**: Networking helps you stay informed about industry trends, competitor movements, and emerging opportunities that can be monetized.

Turning Connections into Clients

Here are some strategies for converting your network into clients or business opportunities:

1. Be Proactive in Communication

Don't wait for opportunities to come to you; take the initiative to reach out to your connections. Regularly engage with your network through email updates, social media interactions, and in-person meetings. Share your latest projects, achievements, or offerings to keep your connections informed about how you can add value.

2. Offer Value First

Before asking for anything in return, focus on providing value to your network. This could be through sharing insightful articles, offering free consultations, or introducing them to others in your network who may benefit from their services. Establishing yourself as a resource increases the likelihood that others will reciprocate.

3. Utilize Social Media

Platforms like LinkedIn are invaluable for networking and business development. Use LinkedIn to showcase your expertise, share content, and engage with your network. Join relevant groups and participate in discussions to increase your visibility and credibility.

4. Host Networking Events

Consider organizing networking events, workshops, or seminars in your area of expertise. This positions you as a leader in your field while giving you the chance to connect with potential clients and collaborators directly. It also helps reinforce relationships within your existing network.

5. Follow Up Strategically

Timely follow-ups after meetings or networking events are crucial. Send personalized messages thanking contacts for their time, reiterating key points discussed, and suggesting next steps. Consistent follow-ups can help turn initial conversations into lasting business relationships.

Networking Tactics for Entrepreneurs

For entrepreneurs, networking is often essential for growth. Here are specific tactics to enhance your networking effectiveness:

1. Create Strategic Partnerships

Look for opportunities to partner with other businesses that complement your services. For example, if you run a marketing agency, consider partnering with a web development company. Together, you can offer comprehensive solutions to clients and refer customers to each other.

2. Leverage Alumni Networks

Your school or university alumni network can be a goldmine for connections. Engage with alumni events, online forums, or social media groups. Alumni are often more willing to support fellow graduates, making it easier to establish rapport and pursue business opportunities.

3. Join Industry Associations

Membership in industry-specific associations or organizations can broaden your network significantly. Attend conferences, workshops, and networking events hosted by these associations to connect with potential clients, suppliers, or mentors.

4. Utilize Online Networking Platforms

In addition to LinkedIn, explore other online platforms dedicated to professional networking. Websites like Meetup can help you find local groups relevant to your industry, while forums and online communities can provide insights and connections across the globe.

5. Develop a Referral Program

Encourage your existing clients to refer new business by implementing a referral program. Offer incentives for successful referrals, such as discounts or rewards. This not only strengthens your relationship with current clients but also expands your network through their connections.

Building Long-Term Relationships

While turning connections into clients is a critical goal, it's essential to focus on building long-term relationships within your network. Here are some tips for maintaining and nurturing these relationships:

1. **Regular Check-Ins**: Schedule periodic check-ins with your connections, even if it's just a quick message to see how they are doing. This keeps you on their radar and reinforces your relationship.
2. **Celebrate Their Successes**: Acknowledge the achievements of your contacts, whether through social media shout-outs or personal messages. Showing genuine interest in their success fosters goodwill and strengthens bonds.
3. **Offer Continuous Support**: Be available to assist your connections whenever possible. Whether it's sharing resources, providing advice, or making introductions, demonstrating your willingness to help can solidify your position as a valuable contact.

Conclusion

Leveraging your network for financial gains requires a proactive approach and a genuine desire to create mutually beneficial relationships. By focusing on providing value, maintaining connections, and exploring collaborative opportunities, you can turn your network into a powerful tool for business growth and financial success. In the next chapter, we will discuss how to build a personal development plan to enhance your career advancement and investment in skills and education.

write chapter 19 for the book Mastering Network and Net Worth Chapter 1: Understanding Networking Definition and significance of networking. Different types of networks (personal, professional, social). Chapter 2: The Psychology of Networking Building trust and rapport. Overcoming networking anxiety. Chapter 3: Identifying Your Networking Goals Assessing personal and professional aspirations. Setting measurable networking objectives. Chapter 4: Building Your Personal Brand Crafting your personal story. Importance of online presence (LinkedIn, social media). Part 2: Expanding Your Network Chapter 5: Where to Network Identifying key networking opportunities (conferences, seminars, online platforms). Leveraging community events and local groups. Chapter 6: The Art of Conversation Effective communication skills. Active listening and engagement techniques. Chapter 7: Follow-Up Strategies Importance of timely follow-ups. Best practices for staying connected. Chapter 8: Building a Diverse Network Benefits of diversity in connections. Strategies for reaching out to different demographics. Part 3: Leveraging Your Network for Success Chapter 9: Networking for Opportunities How to identify and seize opportunities through connections. Case studies of successful networking. Chapter 10: Mentorship and Guidance Finding and nurturing mentor-mentee relationships. The role of mentorship in personal growth. Chapter 11: Collaborative Networking Building partnerships for mutual benefit. Examples of successful collaborations. Chapter 12: Networking Etiquette Dos and don'ts of professional networking. Navigating cultural differences in networking.

Part 4: Understanding Net Worth Chapter 13: Defining Net Worth Assets vs. liabilities: what counts? The importance of tracking your net worth. Chapter 14: Financial Literacy Fundamentals Basic financial concepts everyone should know.

Resources for improving financial literacy. Chapter 15: Creating a Budget and Savings Plan Steps to develop a personal budget. Strategies for saving effectively. Chapter 16: Investing Basics Overview of investment options (stocks, bonds, real estate). Risk assessment and portfolio diversification. Part 5: Increasing Your Net Worth Chapter 17: Income Streams Identifying and creating multiple income sources. Passive income strategies. Chapter 18: Leveraging Networking for Financial Gains How to turn connections into clients or business opportunities. Networking tactics for entrepreneurs. Chapter 19: Building a Personal Development Plan Setting goals for career advancement. Investing in skills and education. Chapter 20: Risk Management and Insurance Importance of protecting your assets. Types of insurance to consider. Part 6: Sustaining Success Chapter 21: Giving Back and Community Engagement The role of philanthropy in networking and net worth. Building a legacy through community involvement. Chapter 22: Adapting to Change Staying relevant in a changing economy. Networking in a digital age. Chapter 23: Continuous Learning and Growth Emphasizing lifelong learning. Resources for ongoing education. Chapter 24: Measuring Your Success Tools for assessing networking and financial growth. Adjusting strategies based on results.

ChatGPT said:

ChatGPT

Chapter 19: Building a Personal Development Plan

A well-crafted personal development plan (PDP) is essential for anyone looking to advance their career, enhance their skills, and increase their net worth. This chapter outlines the steps to create an effective personal development plan, focusing on setting clear goals and investing in your education and skills.

Understanding Personal Development

Personal development is a lifelong process that involves self-improvement in various aspects of life, including professional skills, emotional intelligence, and interpersonal relationships. It's about becoming the best version of yourself, which, in turn, enhances your career prospects and financial opportunities.

The Importance of a Personal Development Plan

A personal development plan provides clarity on where you want to go, how you plan to get there, and the skills you need to develop along the way. Key benefits of having a PDP include:

1. **Goal Clarity**: A well-defined plan helps you articulate your career goals and objectives.
2. **Skill Assessment**: It allows you to evaluate your current skills and identify areas for improvement.
3. **Motivation**: A PDP serves as a roadmap, keeping you motivated and accountable for your progress.
4. **Adaptability**: As circumstances change, a personal development plan can be adjusted to reflect new goals and aspirations.

Steps to Create Your Personal Development Plan

Creating a personal development plan involves several key steps. Here's a structured approach:

1. Self-Assessment

Before setting goals, conduct a thorough self-assessment. This involves:

- **Identifying Strengths and Weaknesses**: Reflect on your skills, experiences, and areas where you excel. Also, recognize your weaknesses and areas for growth.
- **Gathering Feedback**: Seek input from peers, mentors, or supervisors to gain an external perspective on your skills and performance.
- **Evaluating Interests and Values**: Consider what you are passionate about and what values are important to you in your career. This will guide you toward fulfilling opportunities.

2. Set Clear Goals

Once you have a clear understanding of yourself, set specific, measurable, achievable, relevant, and time-bound (SMART) goals.

- **Long-term Goals**: Think about where you want to be in the next five to ten years. This could be a desired job position, a particular skill set, or achieving financial independence.
- **Short-term Goals**: Break your long-term goals into smaller, actionable steps you can achieve within a year.

3. Identify Required Skills and Education

Determine the skills and knowledge necessary to achieve your goals. Consider the following:

- **Technical Skills**: Identify specific technical skills relevant to your industry or desired job.
- **Soft Skills**: Recognize the importance of soft skills such as communication, teamwork, and leadership. These are critical for career advancement.
- **Education and Certifications**: Research educational opportunities, certifications, or workshops that will help you acquire the necessary skills.

4. Create an Action Plan

Develop a detailed action plan that outlines the steps you will take to achieve your goals. This plan should include:

- **Resources Needed**: Identify the resources you need, such as courses, books, or mentorship.
- **Timeline**: Set a timeline for each goal and milestone to keep you accountable.
- **Measurement**: Establish metrics to evaluate your progress. This could include course completion, skill assessments, or feedback from peers.

5. Seek Support and Mentorship

Engage your network for support and guidance. Finding a mentor can be invaluable in your personal development journey. A mentor can provide insights, share experiences, and offer advice on navigating your career path. Consider:

- **Networking for Mentorship**: Use your networking skills to identify potential mentors within your field or through professional organizations.
- **Regular Check-Ins**: Schedule regular meetings with your mentor to discuss progress, challenges, and any adjustments needed in your PDP.

6. Review and Revise Regularly

Personal development is not a one-time activity; it requires ongoing evaluation and adjustment. Schedule regular reviews of your PDP to assess progress and make necessary changes.

- **Reflect on Achievements**: Celebrate your accomplishments and recognize the progress you've made.
- **Adjust Goals**: As your career evolves, your goals and needs may change. Be flexible and willing to revise your plan accordingly.

Investing in Skills and Education

Investing in your education and skills is crucial for long-term career success. Here are strategies to maximize your investment:

1. Continuous Learning

Commit to lifelong learning by staying updated on industry trends and developments. Explore online courses, webinars, and professional conferences to expand your knowledge.

2. Embrace Challenges

Seek out challenging projects at work or in your personal life. This can accelerate your learning and help you develop new skills in real-world scenarios.

3. Networking for Learning Opportunities

Utilize your network to learn about new educational resources, training programs, or job shadowing opportunities. Your connections can be instrumental in providing insights into where to focus your development efforts.

4. Financial Investment in Education

Consider allocating a budget for educational resources. This could include enrolling in courses, purchasing books, or attending conferences. Weigh the potential return on investment (ROI) against the costs to ensure you're making smart choices for your career.

Conclusion

Building a personal development plan is an essential step in achieving your career and financial goals. By conducting a thorough self-assessment, setting clear goals, identifying necessary skills, and actively seeking education and mentorship, you can pave the way for continuous growth and success. In the next chapter, we will explore the importance of risk management and insurance in protecting your assets and ensuring long-term financial security.

4o mini

You said:

write chapter 20 for the book Mastering Network and Net Worth Chapter 1: Understanding Networking Definition and significance of networking. Different types of networks (personal, professional, social). Chapter 2: The Psychology of Networking Building trust and rapport. Overcoming networking anxiety. Chapter 3: Identifying Your Networking Goals Assessing personal and professional aspirations. Setting measurable networking objectives. Chapter 4: Building Your Personal Brand Crafting your personal story. Importance of online presence (LinkedIn, social media). Part 2: Expanding Your Network Chapter 5: Where to Network Identifying key networking opportunities (conferences, seminars, online platforms). Leveraging community events and local groups. Chapter 6: The Art of Conversation Effective communication skills. Active listening and engagement techniques. Chapter 7: Follow-Up Strategies Importance of timely follow-ups. Best practices for staying connected. Chapter 8: Building a Diverse Network Benefits of diversity in connections. Strategies for reaching out to different demographics. Part 3: Leveraging Your Network for Success Chapter 9: Networking for Opportunities How to identify and seize opportunities through connections. Case studies of successful networking. Chapter 10: Mentorship and Guidance Finding and nurturing mentor-mentee relationships. The role of mentorship in personal growth. Chapter 11: Collaborative Networking Building partnerships for mutual benefit. Examples of successful collaborations. Chapter 12: Networking Etiquette Dos and don'ts of professional networking. Navigating cultural differences in networking.

Part 4: Understanding Net Worth Chapter 13: Defining Net Worth Assets vs. liabilities: what counts? The importance of tracking your net worth. Chapter 14: Financial Literacy Fundamentals Basic financial concepts everyone should know.

Resources for improving financial literacy. Chapter 15: Creating a Budget and Savings Plan Steps to develop a personal budget. Strategies for saving effectively. Chapter 16: Investing Basics Overview of investment options (stocks, bonds, real estate). Risk assessment and portfolio diversification. Part 5: Increasing Your Net Worth Chapter 17: Income Streams Identifying and creating multiple income sources. Passive income strategies. Chapter 18: Leveraging Networking for Financial Gains How to turn connections into clients or business opportunities. Networking tactics for entrepreneurs. Chapter 19: Building a Personal Development Plan Setting goals for career advancement. Investing in skills and education. Chapter 20: Risk Management and Insurance Importance of protecting your assets. Types of insurance to consider. Part 6: Sustaining Success Chapter 21: Giving Back and Community Engagement The role of philanthropy in networking and net worth. Building a legacy through community involvement. Chapter 22: Adapting to Change Staying relevant in a changing economy. Networking in a digital age. Chapter 23: Continuous Learning and Growth Emphasizing lifelong learning. Resources for ongoing education. Chapter 24: Measuring Your Success Tools for assessing networking and financial growth. Adjusting strategies based on results.

ChatGPT said:

ChatGPT

Chapter 20: Risk Management and Insurance

In the journey to mastering both your network and net worth, understanding risk management and the role of insurance is paramount. Life is unpredictable, and safeguarding your assets against unforeseen circumstances not only protects your financial standing but also contributes to your overall sense of security and stability. This chapter delves into the importance of protecting your assets and outlines the various types of insurance you should consider.

The Importance of Protecting Your Assets

Every financial decision you make carries some level of risk. Whether you're investing in stocks, starting a business, or purchasing a home, each venture involves uncertainties that could potentially impact your financial health. Effective risk management strategies can help you minimize these risks and safeguard your net worth.

1. Understanding Risk

Risk can be categorized into different types:

- **Personal Risk**: This includes risks associated with health, disability, or even loss of life that could impact your income and expenses.
- **Property Risk**: The risk of losing or damaging physical assets, such as your home, car, or personal belongings.
- **Liability Risk**: The risk of being held legally responsible for damages or injuries to others.
- **Market Risk**: The risk of losing money due to fluctuations in market conditions affecting your investments.

Recognizing these risks allows you to take proactive steps to manage them effectively.

2. The Financial Impact of Not Managing Risk

Failing to manage risk can lead to significant financial consequences, such as:

- **Loss of Income**: An unexpected illness or injury can result in lost wages, affecting your ability to cover expenses and save for the future.
- **Asset Depletion**: Without adequate insurance, a single event like a natural disaster or accident can wipe out your savings and assets.
- **Increased Liability**: If you don't protect yourself against liability risks, you may face lawsuits that can drain your financial resources.

Types of Insurance to Consider

Insurance serves as a financial safety net, allowing you to mitigate risks and protect your assets. Here are the primary types of insurance to consider:

1. Health Insurance

Health insurance is essential for protecting yourself against high medical costs resulting from illness or injury. It helps cover medical expenses, including hospital visits, surgeries, and preventive care. Consider the following:

- **Types of Plans**: Understand the different types of health plans available, such as employer-sponsored insurance, individual plans, and government programs like Medicare and Medicaid.
- **Coverage Details**: Review the coverage details, including premiums, deductibles, copayments, and out-of-pocket maximums.

2. Life Insurance

Life insurance is crucial if you have dependents or financial obligations. It provides a financial safety net for your loved ones in the event of your passing. Key points to consider:

- **Term Life vs. Whole Life**: Understand the difference between term life insurance (coverage for a specific period) and whole life insurance (coverage for your lifetime).
- **Coverage Amount**: Determine how much coverage you need based on your financial obligations and future goals.

3. Disability Insurance

Disability insurance protects your income if you become unable to work due to illness or injury. This is especially important if you're self-employed or your income is your primary support. Types to consider:

- **Short-Term Disability**: Covers a portion of your income for a limited period (typically 3-6 months).
- **Long-Term Disability**: Provides coverage for an extended period, sometimes until retirement age.

4. Homeowners or Renters Insurance

This insurance protects your property and personal belongings against risks like fire, theft, or natural disasters. Considerations include:

- **Homeowners Insurance**: If you own a home, this covers damage to your property and liability for injuries that occur on your property.
- **Renters Insurance**: If you rent, this protects your personal belongings and may include liability coverage.

5. Auto Insurance

Auto insurance is mandatory in most places and protects you against financial loss in case of an accident or theft. Key aspects to consider:

- **Liability Coverage**: Covers damages you cause to others in an accident.
- **Collision Coverage**: Covers damages to your vehicle resulting from a collision.
- **Comprehensive Coverage**: Covers non-collision-related damages, such as theft or natural disasters.

6. Liability Insurance

Liability insurance protects you from legal claims against you, covering legal fees and damages awarded. Types to consider:

- **Personal Liability**: Covers claims for bodily injury or property damage you may cause to others.
- **Professional Liability**: Also known as malpractice insurance, this is essential for professionals like doctors, lawyers, and consultants.

Creating a Risk Management Strategy

To effectively protect your assets, consider implementing a risk management strategy that includes:

1. **Assessing Your Risks**: Regularly evaluate your personal and financial situation to identify potential risks you may face.
2. **Establishing Coverage Needs**: Determine the types and amounts of insurance you need based on your risk assessment.
3. **Reviewing Policies Regularly**: Periodically review your insurance policies to ensure they still meet your needs as your life circumstances change.
4. **Consulting Professionals**: Work with financial advisors and insurance agents to help you navigate the complexities of insurance and risk management.

Conclusion

Protecting your assets through effective risk management and appropriate insurance coverage is vital for achieving long-term financial stability and peace of mind. By understanding the different types of risks and corresponding insurance options, you can make informed decisions that safeguard your network and net worth. In the next chapter, we will explore the role of philanthropy in networking and how giving back can enhance both your personal and professional life.

4o mini

You said:

write chapter 21 for the book Mastering Network and Net Worth Chapter 1: Understanding Networking Definition and significance of networking. Different types of networks (personal, professional, social). Chapter 2: The Psychology of Networking Building trust and rapport. Overcoming networking anxiety. Chapter 3: Identifying Your Networking Goals Assessing personal and professional aspirations. Setting measurable networking objectives. Chapter 4: Building Your Personal Brand Crafting your personal story. Importance of online presence (LinkedIn, social media). Part 2: Expanding Your Network Chapter 5: Where to Network Identifying key networking opportunities (conferences, seminars, online platforms). Leveraging community events and local groups. Chapter 6: The Art of Conversation Effective communication skills. Active listening and engagement techniques. Chapter 7: Follow-Up Strategies Importance of timely follow-ups. Best practices for staying connected. Chapter 8: Building a Diverse Network Benefits of diversity in connections. Strategies for reaching out to different demographics. Part 3: Leveraging Your Network for Success Chapter 9: Networking for Opportunities How to identify and seize opportunities through connections. Case studies of successful networking. Chapter 10: Mentorship and Guidance Finding and nurturing mentor-mentee relationships. The role of mentorship in personal growth. Chapter 11: Collaborative Networking Building partnerships for mutual benefit. Examples of successful collaborations. Chapter 12: Networking Etiquette Dos and don'ts of professional networking. Navigating cultural differences in networking.

Part 4: Understanding Net Worth Chapter 13: Defining Net Worth Assets vs. liabilities: what counts? The importance of tracking your net worth. Chapter 14: Financial Literacy Fundamentals Basic financial concepts everyone should know.

Resources for improving financial literacy. Chapter 15: Creating a Budget and Savings Plan Steps to develop a personal budget. Strategies for saving effectively. Chapter 16: Investing Basics Overview of investment options (stocks, bonds, real estate). Risk assessment and portfolio diversification. Part 5: Increasing Your Net Worth Chapter 17: Income Streams Identifying and creating multiple income sources. Passive income strategies. Chapter 18: Leveraging Networking for Financial Gains How to turn connections into clients or business opportunities. Networking tactics for entrepreneurs. Chapter 19: Building a Personal Development Plan Setting goals for career advancement. Investing in skills and education. Chapter 20: Risk Management and Insurance Importance of protecting your assets. Types of insurance to consider. Part 6: Sustaining Success Chapter 21: Giving Back and Community Engagement The role of philanthropy in networking and net worth. Building a legacy through community involvement. Chapter 22: Adapting to Change Staying relevant in a changing economy. Networking in a digital age. Chapter 23: Continuous Learning and Growth Emphasizing lifelong learning. Resources for ongoing education. Chapter 24: Measuring Your Success Tools for assessing networking and financial growth. Adjusting strategies based on results.

ChatGPT said:

ChatGPT

Chapter 21: Giving Back and Community Engagement

In the pursuit of mastering networking and building net worth, one essential component often overlooked is the role of giving back. Philanthropy and community engagement not only contribute to the well-being of others but also enhance your own network and financial growth. This chapter explores how giving back can lead to meaningful connections, greater influence, and a lasting legacy.

The Role of Philanthropy in Networking

Philanthropy goes beyond financial contributions; it embodies a commitment to positively impacting society. Engaging in charitable activities can expand your network in several significant ways:

1. Building Trust and Credibility

When you actively participate in philanthropic efforts, you demonstrate values such as compassion, responsibility, and a desire to make a difference. This can enhance your reputation and build trust among peers, clients, and potential business partners. People are more likely to connect with and support individuals who they perceive as altruistic and community-oriented.

2. Creating Meaningful Connections

Philanthropy often brings together individuals from diverse backgrounds with shared interests and values. Participating in community service, charity events, or fundraising initiatives allows you to meet like-minded people who may become valuable connections in your personal and professional life.

3. Expanding Your Influence

Engaging in philanthropy can increase your visibility within your community and industry. As you become known for your contributions and commitment to social causes, you may find that others seek your insights and expertise. This can lead to speaking opportunities, collaboration on projects, and other networking advantages.

Building a Legacy Through Community Involvement

Community engagement not only benefits your network but also allows you to leave a lasting legacy. Consider the following aspects of building a legacy through giving back:

1. Aligning with Your Values

Identify causes that resonate with your personal values and interests. Whether it's education, environmental conservation, health care, or social justice, supporting initiatives that align with your beliefs will make your contributions more meaningful and fulfilling.

2. Engaging with Local Organizations

Start by engaging with local nonprofits, community organizations, or grassroots initiatives. This can provide you with opportunities to volunteer your time, skills, and resources, fostering connections with individuals who share your passion for making a difference.

3. Establishing Your Own Initiatives

If you have the resources and commitment, consider establishing your own charitable initiative or foundation. This can enhance your influence in the community and create a platform for your philanthropic goals. It can also serve as a legacy project that reflects your values and aspirations.

The Practical Benefits of Giving Back

In addition to the intrinsic rewards of philanthropy, there are practical benefits to giving back that can enhance your net worth:

1. Tax Benefits

Contributions to qualified charitable organizations can provide tax deductions, allowing you to reduce your taxable income. Understanding the tax implications of your philanthropic efforts can lead to significant savings.

2. Enhanced Professional Opportunities

Philanthropic involvement can lead to professional advantages. Business leaders and entrepreneurs often find that their commitment to social causes can open doors to new clients, partnerships, and business ventures. People prefer to work with those who have a genuine commitment to improving the world around them.

3. Strengthening Employee Relations

If you are a business owner or manager, encouraging employees to engage in community service can boost morale, enhance teamwork, and improve employee retention. Companies that prioritize philanthropy often attract talent that shares their values, creating a positive work culture that can contribute to overall success.

Developing a Philanthropic Strategy

To effectively integrate giving back into your networking and personal development plan, consider the following steps:

1. Define Your Philanthropic Goals

Clarify what you hope to achieve through your philanthropic efforts. Whether it's financial support for a specific cause, volunteer time, or raising awareness about an issue, having clear goals will guide your actions.

2. Research Organizations

Take the time to research and identify organizations that align with your values and goals. Evaluate their impact, transparency, and effectiveness to ensure that your contributions make a meaningful difference.

3. Create a Giving Plan

Develop a structured giving plan that outlines your budget for charitable contributions, time commitments for volunteering, and specific initiatives you want to support. This will help you stay organized and focused in your philanthropic efforts.

4. Network with Other Philanthropists

Connect with other individuals and organizations involved in philanthropy. Attend charity events, join boards of nonprofits, and seek mentorship from established philanthropists. These connections can provide insights, resources, and opportunities to amplify your impact.

5. Measure Your Impact

Regularly assess the impact of your philanthropic efforts. Reflect on how your contributions have benefited your chosen causes and the connections you've made along the way. Adjust your strategy as needed to ensure that your giving remains aligned with your values and goals.

Conclusion

Giving back and engaging in community initiatives is not only a moral imperative but also a strategic approach to enhancing your network and net worth. By aligning your philanthropic efforts with your personal and professional goals, you can create meaningful connections, build a legacy, and leave a lasting impact on the world. As we transition to the next chapter, we will explore how to adapt to change in a dynamic economy, emphasizing the importance of staying relevant and innovative in your networking efforts.

Chapter 22: Sustaining Your Network for Lifelong Net Worth

By the time you reach this final chapter, you have journeyed through the fundamentals of networking, explored the psychology behind meaningful connections, set measurable goals, built a personal brand, expanded your circle, leveraged relationships for opportunity, and learned the etiquette that keeps doors open. Chapter 22 is about what comes next — the long game. Because a network is not a one-time achievement; it is a living ecosystem that must be nurtured, refreshed, and aligned with the evolving seasons of your life and career.

The Lifelong Mindset

Many people treat networking as a transactional activity — something you do when you need a job, a client, or an introduction. The truly successful networkers, however, treat their network as a garden. They water it consistently, prune what no longer serves, plant new seeds, and never wait until harvest time to start tending. The result is a web of relationships that compounds in value over decades, producing opportunities, wisdom, friendship, and yes — net worth — at every stage of life.

The lifelong mindset rests on three principles:

1. **Consistency over intensity.** A five-minute message every month is worth more than a three-hour reunion every five years.
2. **Generosity before need.** Give value when you want nothing; you will receive value when you need everything.
3. **Curiosity as fuel.** The moment you stop being curious about people is the moment your network stops growing.

Auditing Your Network Annually

Just as you review your finances at the end of each year, you should audit your relational capital. Set aside a few hours once a year to ask:

- Who are the ten people who have most influenced my growth in the past twelve months?
- Whom have I lost touch with that I genuinely value?
- Which connections drain me, and which energize me?
- Where are the gaps — industries, skill sets, generations, geographies — in my network?
- Whom did I help this year, and whom did I fail to help when I could have?

This audit is not about ranking people by usefulness. It is about taking honest stock of where you have invested your time and attention, and recalibrating if necessary.

Reactivating Dormant Ties

Sociologists have long observed that *dormant ties* — relationships that once were close but have faded — are often more valuable than either close friends or brand-new contacts. Dormant ties bring novel information, fresh perspectives, and a foundation of trust that does not need to be rebuilt from scratch.

To reactivate a dormant tie:

- Lead with sincerity, not agenda. "I was thinking of you today because…" is far more powerful than "I need a favor."
- Reference a shared memory or mutual connection.
- Offer something — an article, an introduction, a congratulations — before asking for anything.
- Suggest a low-pressure next step: a 20-minute call, a coffee if geography allows, or simply an ongoing exchange of messages.

Evolving With Your Network

As you grow, your network should grow with you — and sometimes ahead of you. If every person in your circle is at your current level or below, you will plateau. If every person is dramatically above you, you will feel perpetually out of place. Aim for a healthy mix: peers who understand your daily reality, mentors who see further than you can, and mentees who keep you sharp, humble, and connected to the next generation.

Revisit the goals you set in Chapter 3. They have likely changed. Your network should reflect who you are becoming, not only who you have been.

Passing It On

The ultimate measure of a mastered network is not what it has given you — it is what it has enabled you to give others. The introductions you make, the mentees you guide, the collaborations you spark, and the doors you hold open for people who would otherwise be locked out — these are the dividends of a life well networked.

When you open doors for others, you become the kind of person others want in their network. The cycle renews itself, and your net worth — measured not only in dollars but in trust, influence, and impact — continues to compound long after any single transaction is forgotten.

Final Reflection

Mastering network and net worth is not about collecting business cards, inflating follower counts, or strategically positioning yourself at the right event. It is about becoming a person of integrity, generosity, and presence — someone whose relationships are deep, diverse, and durable.

Close this book and look at your phone, your inbox, your calendar. Somewhere in there is a person you have been meaning to reach out to. Send that message today. That single act, repeated over a lifetime, is what mastery looks like.

Your network is your net worth. Tend it well, and it will carry you — and the people you love — further than any balance sheet ever could.

Part 4: Understanding Net Worth Chapter 13: Defining Net Worth Assets vs. liabilities: what counts? The importance of tracking your net worth. Chapter 14: Financial Literacy Fundamentals Basic financial concepts everyone should know.

Resources for improving financial literacy. Chapter 15: Creating a Budget and Savings Plan Steps to develop a personal budget. Strategies for saving effectively. Chapter 16: Investing Basics Overview of investment options (stocks, bonds, real estate). Risk assessment and portfolio diversification. Part 5: Increasing Your Net Worth Chapter 17: Income Streams Identifying and creating multiple income sources. Passive income strategies. Chapter 18: Leveraging Networking for Financial Gains How to turn connections into clients or business opportunities. Networking tactics for entrepreneurs. Chapter 19: Building a Personal Development Plan Setting goals for career advancement. Investing in skills and education. Chapter 20: Risk Management and Insurance Importance of protecting your assets. Types of insurance to consider. Part 6: Sustaining Success Chapter 21: Giving Back and Community Engagement The role of philanthropy in networking and net worth. Building a legacy through community involvement. Chapter 22: Adapting to Change Staying relevant in a changing economy. Networking in a digital age. Chapter 23: Continuous Learning and Growth Emphasizing lifelong learning. Resources for ongoing education. Chapter 24: Measuring Your Success Tools for assessing networking and financial growth. Adjusting strategies based on results.

ChatGPT said:

ChatGPT

Chapter 22: Adapting to Change

In an ever-evolving world, the ability to adapt is not just a survival skill; it's a necessity for success in both networking and financial growth. As economic landscapes shift and technological advancements accelerate, staying relevant becomes paramount. This chapter explores strategies to adapt to change effectively, emphasizing the importance of networking in a digital age.

Staying Relevant in a Changing Economy

The modern economy is characterized by rapid change. Industries transform, new markets emerge, and consumer preferences evolve. Here are key strategies to remain relevant:

1. Embrace Continuous Learning

Lifelong learning is essential to adapt to new challenges and opportunities. Consider the following approaches:

- **Online Courses and Webinars:** Platforms like Coursera, Udemy, and LinkedIn Learning offer courses on various subjects, including technology trends, financial literacy, and personal development. Regularly enroll in relevant courses to keep your skills sharp.
- **Podcasts and Audiobooks:** Utilize commute or downtime to absorb knowledge through podcasts and audiobooks. These resources can provide insights from industry leaders and thought-provoking discussions on contemporary topics.
- **Networking Events:** Attend workshops, seminars, and conferences focused on emerging trends in your industry. These events can provide both learning and networking opportunities.

2. Stay Informed About Industry Trends

Keeping a pulse on industry developments will help you anticipate changes. Here's how:

- **Follow Industry Leaders:** Subscribe to newsletters, follow influencers, and engage with experts on social media. Platforms like Twitter and LinkedIn are excellent for real-time updates and insights.
- **Join Professional Associations:** Many industries have organizations that provide resources, networking opportunities, and access to the latest research. Membership can keep you informed about industry standards and innovations.
- **Participate in Discussion Forums:** Engaging in online forums and communities (such as Reddit or industry-specific groups) allows you to share knowledge and gain perspectives from peers facing similar challenges.

3. Cultivate Adaptability

Developing a mindset that embraces change is crucial. Here are practical ways to enhance your adaptability:

- **Be Open to Feedback:** Constructive criticism can guide your growth. Seek feedback from mentors, peers, and even clients to identify areas for improvement.
- **Experiment and Innovate:** Don't hesitate to try new approaches in your professional endeavors. Experimentation can lead to breakthroughs and new opportunities.
- **Practice Resilience:** Challenges and setbacks are inevitable. Focus on building resilience by developing coping strategies, such as mindfulness or stress management techniques.

Networking in a Digital Age

As the digital landscape expands, networking has evolved dramatically. Understanding how to navigate this new terrain is essential for maintaining and growing your network.

1. Leverage Online Networking Platforms

Digital networking platforms like LinkedIn, Twitter, and industry-specific forums offer unique opportunities to connect. Consider the following strategies:

- **Optimize Your Online Presence:** Ensure your profiles on networking platforms reflect your personal brand. Use professional photos, craft compelling summaries, and showcase your skills and achievements.
- **Engage Actively:** Participate in discussions, share valuable content, and comment on posts to establish yourself as an expert in your field. Engaging with others can lead to new connections and opportunities.
- **Utilize Virtual Events:** Webinars, online conferences, and virtual networking events are now commonplace. Attend these events to connect with others while expanding your knowledge.

2. Personalize Your Outreach

In a digital age, generic messages can easily be overlooked. Personalization is key to effective networking:

- **Research Before Reaching Out:** Before contacting someone, take time to research their background and interests. Tailor your message to reflect your understanding of their work and how you can collaborate or add value.
- **Follow Up Thoughtfully:** After connecting, send a follow-up message expressing appreciation and suggesting potential areas of collaboration. This reinforces the relationship and keeps the lines of communication open.

3. Build a Strong Personal Brand Online

Your online presence is a crucial part of your networking strategy:

- **Create Valuable Content:** Share articles, videos, or insights that align with your expertise. Consistent, high-quality content can attract attention and establish you as a thought leader in your field.
- **Engage with Influencers:** Connect and interact with influencers and industry leaders. Sharing their content and providing thoughtful commentary can help you get noticed and foster relationships.
- **Maintain Professionalism:** Remember that online interactions are often permanent. Be mindful of your digital footprint, and ensure your online behavior aligns with your personal brand.

Conclusion

Adapting to change is essential for success in today's dynamic environment. By embracing continuous learning, staying informed about industry trends, and cultivating adaptability, you position yourself to thrive amid uncertainty. Additionally, leveraging digital networking tools effectively will expand your connections and opportunities, ensuring that you remain relevant in your field.

As we move into the next chapter, we will delve into the importance of continuous learning and growth, emphasizing how to create a sustainable strategy for lifelong education and personal development.

4o mini

You said:

Chapter 23: Sustaining Your Network Over a Lifetime

Networks, like gardens, require continuous care. The connections you build today will only bear fruit tomorrow if you invest the time, attention, and intentionality necessary to keep them alive. In this final chapter, we turn our focus to the long game: how to sustain, refresh, and evolve your network over the course of a lifetime so that it continues to grow in both reach and net worth.

The Long View of Networking

Most people think of networking as a series of transactions — meet someone, exchange cards, ask for a favor. But the truly powerful networks are those that compound over decades. A classmate from university may become a CEO twenty years later. A junior colleague you mentored may one day sit on a board that can open doors for you. The relationships you nurture in your twenties, thirties, and forties become the scaffolding of your opportunities in your fifties, sixties, and beyond.

Sustaining a network means shifting your mindset from short-term gain to long-term stewardship. It means treating every relationship as an investment that appreciates with time, attention, and authenticity.

Principles of Lifelong Network Maintenance

1. Consistency Over Intensity. It is far better to reach out to a contact twice a year for twenty years than to engage intensely for six months and disappear. Small, regular gestures — a thoughtful message, a shared article, a birthday note — build durable bonds.

2. Give Before You Ask. The healthiest networks operate on reciprocity, but the most respected nodes within them are those who give generously without expectation. Offer introductions, share insights, celebrate others' wins publicly.

3. Keep Your Records Alive. A customer-relationship-management (CRM) approach to personal contacts is not cold or calculating — it is respectful. Track who you know, when you last connected, what matters to them, and what you promised to do. Systems protect relationships from the erosion of memory.

4. Refresh and Prune. Networks, like wardrobes, benefit from periodic editing. Some connections naturally fade; forcing them drains energy. Others deserve renewed investment. Audit your network annually and ask: which relationships do I want to deepen this year?

Navigating Life's Transitions

Careers change. People move cities, switch industries, retire, re-enter the workforce, or start over entirely. Each transition tests the resilience of your network. The contacts who stand by you during a career change or a personal setback are the ones you invested in before you needed them.

When you face a transition, be transparent with your network. Share your next chapter. Ask for advice, not just opportunities. And when a contact in your network is going through their own transition, be the person who shows up — not because it serves you, but because it is the right thing to do.

Passing the Network Forward

A mature networker does not hoard connections — they broker them. The highest expression of networking mastery is becoming a connector: someone who introduces the right people to one another, multiplying value across the community. When you become known as a trusted connector, opportunities flow toward you effortlessly, because you have become indispensable to the flow of opportunity itself.

Consider also the legacy dimension. Who are you bringing up behind you? Mentorship, championing younger professionals, and opening doors for those without access are not only ethical imperatives — they are how networks replenish themselves generationally.

The Intersection of Network and Net Worth

Throughout this book, we have drawn the connection between the quality of your relationships and the quality of your life — financial, professional, and personal. Net worth, in its fullest sense, is not merely what you own. It is who you know, who knows you, who trusts you, and who will stand beside you when circumstances shift.

A thriving network amplifies every other form of capital you possess. It turns knowledge into opportunity, opportunity into income, and income into lasting wealth. It converts isolation into belonging and ambition into achievement.

A Final Word

The work of networking is never finished. Relationships are not built; they are being built. The habits, mindsets, and practices in this book are not a checklist to complete — they are a way of moving through the world.

Begin today. Reach out to one person you have lost touch with. Introduce two people who should know each other. Thank a mentor who shaped your trajectory. In doing so, you affirm the simple truth at the heart of this book: your network is your net worth, and it grows every time you choose to show up for someone else.

The story of your network is still being written. Make it one worth telling.

Part 4: Understanding Net Worth

Chapter 13: Defining Net Worth
Assets vs. liabilities: what counts? The importance of tracking your net worth.

Chapter 14: Financial Literacy Fundamentals
Basic financial concepts everyone should know. Resources for improving financial literacy.

Chapter 15: Creating a Budget and Savings Plan
Steps to develop a personal budget. Strategies for saving effectively.

Chapter 16: Investing Basics
Overview of investment options (stocks, bonds, real estate). Risk assessment and portfolio diversification.

Part 5: Increasing Your Net Worth

Chapter 17: Income Streams
Identifying and creating multiple income sources. Passive income strategies.

Chapter 18: Leveraging Networking for Financial Gains
How to turn connections into clients or business opportunities. Networking tactics for entrepreneurs.

Chapter 19: Building a Personal Development Plan
Setting goals for career advancement. Investing in skills and education.

Chapter 20: Risk Management and Insurance
Importance of protecting your assets. Types of insurance to consider.

Part 6: Sustaining Success

Chapter 21: Giving Back and Community Engagement
The role of philanthropy in networking and net worth. Building a legacy through community involvement.

Chapter 22: Adapting to Change
Staying relevant in a changing economy. Networking in a digital age.

Chapter 23: Continuous Learning and Growth
Emphasizing lifelong learning. Resources for ongoing education.

Chapter 24: Measuring Your Success
Tools for assessing networking and financial growth. Adjusting strategies based on results.

ChatGPT

Thought for a couple of seconds

Chapter 23: Continuous Learning and Growth

In the pursuit of mastering your network and increasing your net worth, one principle remains steadfast: the importance of continuous learning and personal growth. The world is constantly evolving, driven by technological advancements, shifting market dynamics, and changing societal norms. To stay ahead and maintain relevance, it is essential to commit to lifelong learning and personal development. This chapter explores the significance of continuous learning, strategies to foster personal growth, and resources to support your ongoing education journey.

The Importance of Lifelong Learning

1. Staying Competitive

In a rapidly changing job market, the skills and knowledge you possess today may become obsolete tomorrow. Continuous learning ensures that you remain competitive by keeping your skills up-to-date and relevant. This adaptability is crucial for career advancement and for seizing new opportunities as they arise.

2. Enhancing Personal Growth

Personal development goes beyond professional skills. It encompasses emotional intelligence, leadership abilities, and interpersonal skills. Continuous learning fosters self-awareness, resilience, and the ability to navigate complex social dynamics, all of which contribute to both personal and professional success.

3. Driving Innovation

Continuous learners are often the drivers of innovation within organizations. By staying informed about the latest trends and technologies, you can bring fresh ideas and perspectives to your work, leading to improved processes, products, and services.

4. Increasing Financial Opportunities

Investing in your education and skills can lead to higher earning potential. Advanced skills and certifications often translate to better job positions, higher salaries, and more lucrative business opportunities, directly impacting your net worth.

Strategies for Continuous Learning

1. Set Clear Learning Goals

Establish specific, measurable, achievable, relevant, and time-bound (SMART) goals for your learning journey. Whether it's mastering a new software tool, obtaining a certification, or developing leadership skills, clear goals provide direction and motivation.

Example Goals:

- Complete an online course in digital marketing within six months.
- Attend at least three industry conferences this year.
- Read one business-related book each month.

2. Create a Learning Schedule

Allocate dedicated time for learning in your daily or weekly schedule. Consistency is key to making steady progress. Whether it's setting aside an hour each morning for reading or dedicating weekends to online courses, a structured schedule helps integrate learning into your routine.

3. Embrace Diverse Learning Methods

Different methods of learning can cater to various preferences and enhance retention. Explore a mix of the following:

- **Formal Education**: Enroll in degree programs, certifications, or specialized courses.
- **Online Learning**: Utilize platforms like Coursera, Udemy, LinkedIn Learning, and Khan Academy for flexible learning options.
- **Workshops and Seminars**: Participate in hands-on workshops and seminars to gain practical experience.
- **Reading and Research**: Stay informed by reading books, journals, and industry publications.
- **Podcasts and Webinars**: Listen to experts discuss relevant topics while on the go.

4. Apply What You Learn

Practical application reinforces learning and solidifies knowledge. Seek opportunities to implement new skills and concepts in your daily work or personal projects. This could involve volunteering for new projects at work, starting a side business, or mentoring others.

5. Seek Feedback and Reflect

Regularly seek feedback from peers, mentors, and supervisors to gauge your progress and identify areas for improvement. Reflecting on your experiences helps you understand what works, what doesn't, and how you can adjust your strategies for better outcomes.

6. Join Learning Communities

Engage with communities of like-minded individuals who share your commitment to learning. Online forums, social media groups, and local meetups provide platforms to exchange ideas, seek advice, and collaborate on learning initiatives.

Resources for Ongoing Education

1. Online Learning Platforms

- **Coursera**: Offers courses from top universities and companies, covering a wide range of subjects.
- **Udemy**: Provides affordable courses on various topics, including business, technology, and personal development.
- **LinkedIn Learning**: Features professional courses that integrate with your LinkedIn profile, making it easy to showcase new skills.
- **Khan Academy**: A free resource offering lessons in many subjects, particularly useful for foundational knowledge.

2. Books and Publications

- **Business Classics**: Titles like *"The 7 Habits of Highly Effective People"* by Stephen R. Covey and *"Thinking, Fast and Slow"* by Daniel Kahneman offer timeless insights.
- **Industry-Specific Books**: Stay updated with the latest trends and innovations in your field by reading contemporary works.
- **Magazines and Journals**: Subscriptions to publications like *Harvard Business Review* or *Forbes* can keep you informed about industry developments.

3. Podcasts and Webinars

- **Podcasts**: Listen to shows like *"The Tim Ferriss Show"*, *"How I Built This"*, and *"The Knowledge Project"* for interviews with successful individuals and deep dives into various topics.
- **Webinars**: Attend live webinars hosted by industry experts to gain real-time insights and ask questions.

4. Professional Associations and Organizations

Joining professional bodies related to your industry can provide access to exclusive resources, training programs, and networking opportunities. Examples include the American Marketing Association (AMA), Project Management Institute (PMI), and the National Association of Realtors (NAR).

5. Local Workshops and Seminars

Participate in workshops and seminars offered by local community colleges, universities, and training centers. These events often provide hands-on experience and opportunities to network with other learners and professionals.

6. Mentorship Programs

Engage in mentorship programs where experienced professionals can guide your learning and development. Mentors can provide personalized advice, share their experiences, and help you navigate your career path.

Overcoming Barriers to Continuous Learning
1. Time Constraints

Balancing work, personal life, and learning can be challenging. Prioritize your learning goals and integrate them into your daily routine. Even small, consistent efforts can lead to significant progress over time.

2. Financial Limitations

While some educational resources can be expensive, there are plenty of free or affordable options available. Utilize public libraries, free online courses, and community resources to continue learning without breaking the bank.

3. Lack of Motivation

Stay motivated by setting clear goals, tracking your progress, and celebrating your achievements. Surround yourself with supportive individuals who encourage your learning endeavors.

4. Information Overload

With the abundance of information available, it's easy to feel overwhelmed. Focus on quality over quantity by selecting resources that align with your goals and eliminating distractions.

Conclusion

Continuous learning and personal growth are indispensable for mastering your network and enhancing your net worth. By committing to lifelong learning, setting clear goals, utilizing diverse resources, and overcoming common barriers, you can stay ahead in a dynamic world. Embrace the journey of personal development, and you will not only achieve financial success but also lead a more fulfilling and empowered life. In the final chapter, we will discuss the tools and methods for measuring your success, ensuring that your efforts lead to tangible results.

o1-mini

You said:

write chapter 24 for the book Mastering Network and Net Worth Chapter 1: Understanding Networking Definition and significance of networking. Different types of networks (personal, professional, social). Chapter 2: The Psychology of Networking Building trust and rapport. Overcoming networking anxiety. Chapter 3: Identifying Your Networking Goals Assessing personal and professional aspirations. Setting measurable networking objectives. Chapter 4: Building Your Personal Brand Crafting your personal story. Importance of online presence (LinkedIn, social media). Part 2: Expanding Your Network Chapter 5: Where to Network Identifying key networking opportunities (conferences, seminars, online platforms). Leveraging community events and local groups. Chapter 6: The Art of Conversation Effective communication skills. Active listening and engagement techniques. Chapter 7: Follow-Up Strategies Importance of timely follow-ups. Best practices for staying connected. Chapter 8: Building a Diverse Network Benefits of diversity in connections. Strategies for reaching out to different demographics. Part 3: Leveraging Your Network for Success Chapter 9: Networking for Opportunities How to identify and seize opportunities through connections. Case studies of successful networking. Chapter 10: Mentorship and Guidance Finding and nurturing mentor-mentee relationships. The role of mentorship in personal growth. Chapter 11: Collaborative Networking Building partnerships for mutual benefit. Examples of successful collaborations. Chapter 12: Networking Etiquette Dos and don'ts of professional networking. Navigating cultural differences in networking.

Part 4: Understanding Net Worth Chapter 13: Defining Net Worth Assets vs. liabilities: what counts? The importance of tracking your net worth. Chapter 14: Financial Literacy Fundamentals Basic financial concepts everyone should know.

Resources for improving financial literacy. Chapter 15: Creating a Budget and Savings Plan Steps to develop a personal budget. Strategies for saving effectively. Chapter 16: Investing Basics Overview of investment options (stocks, bonds, real estate). Risk assessment and portfolio diversification. Part 5: Increasing Your Net Worth Chapter 17: Income Streams Identifying and creating multiple income sources. Passive income strategies. Chapter 18: Leveraging Networking for Financial Gains How to turn connections into clients or business opportunities. Networking tactics for entrepreneurs. Chapter 19: Building a Personal Development Plan Setting goals for career advancement. Investing in skills and education. Chapter 20: Risk Management and Insurance Importance of protecting your assets. Types of insurance to consider. Part 6: Sustaining Success Chapter 21: Giving Back and Community Engagement The role of philanthropy in networking and net worth. Building a legacy through community involvement. Chapter 22: Adapting to Change Staying relevant in a changing economy. Networking in a digital age. Chapter 23: Continuous Learning and Growth Emphasizing lifelong learning. Resources for ongoing education. Chapter 24: Measuring Your Success Tools for assessing networking and financial growth. Adjusting strategies based on results.

ChatGPT

Thought for a few seconds

Chapter 24: Measuring Your Success

Achieving mastery in networking and enhancing your net worth requires not only strategic action but also the ability to measure and evaluate your progress. Without effective measurement, it's challenging to determine whether your efforts are yielding the desired results or to identify areas that need improvement. This chapter delves into the tools and methodologies for assessing both your networking achievements and financial growth, and outlines strategies for adjusting your plans based on the insights gained.

The Importance of Measuring Success

Understanding how to measure success is crucial for several reasons:

1. **Accountability**: Tracking your progress keeps you accountable to your goals and commitments.
2. **Informed Decision-Making**: Data-driven insights enable you to make informed adjustments to your strategies.
3. **Motivation**: Visible progress can boost your motivation and sustain your momentum.
4. **Identifying Strengths and Weaknesses**: Regular assessment helps you recognize what's working and what needs improvement.

Tools for Assessing Networking Growth

Effective networking is both an art and a science. Measuring its success involves both quantitative and qualitative assessments. Here are the primary tools and metrics to consider:

1. Quantitative Metrics

Quantitative metrics provide measurable data that can indicate the breadth and effectiveness of your networking efforts.

- **Number of New Connections**: Track the number of new contacts you add to your network within a specific timeframe.
- **Frequency of Interactions**: Measure how often you engage with your network through meetings, emails, calls, or social media interactions.
- **Event Participation**: Count the number of networking events, conferences, or seminars you attend.
- **Referral Rate**: Monitor the number of referrals or introductions you receive from your network.

2. Qualitative Metrics

Qualitative metrics offer insights into the quality and depth of your relationships.

- **Relationship Strength**: Assess the depth of your connections—are they casual acquaintances or meaningful, mutually beneficial relationships?
- **Engagement Quality**: Evaluate the level of engagement in your interactions. Are conversations substantive and collaborative?
- **Value Exchange**: Consider how much value you and your contacts are providing to each other. Are you both benefiting from the relationship?
- **Trust and Rapport**: Gauge the level of trust and rapport you have built with your network.

3. Networking Tools and Software

Utilizing the right tools can streamline the process of tracking and analyzing your networking efforts.

- **Customer Relationship Management (CRM) Systems**: Tools like Salesforce, HubSpot, or Zoho CRM help manage and track interactions with your contacts.
- **Networking Apps**: Applications like LinkedIn, Shapr, and Bumble Bizz offer features to track your connections and engagement.
- **Spreadsheets**: Customized spreadsheets can be tailored to track specific networking metrics relevant to your goals.

Tools for Assessing Financial Growth

Monitoring your financial growth is essential to ensure that your strategies are effective and that you're on track to achieve your financial goals. Here are the key tools and metrics to consider:

1. Net Worth Trackers

Net worth is a comprehensive measure of your financial health. Tracking it regularly helps you understand your financial position.

- **Personal Finance Software**: Tools like Personal Capital, Mint, and Quicken automatically track your assets and liabilities, providing real-time net worth calculations.
- **Spreadsheets**: For those who prefer a hands-on approach, spreadsheets can be customized to list all assets and liabilities, calculating net worth manually.

2. Budgeting Tools

Effective budgeting is foundational to financial growth. These tools help you manage your income and expenses efficiently.

- **Budgeting Apps**: Applications such as YNAB (You Need A Budget), EveryDollar, and PocketGuard offer user-friendly interfaces to create and monitor budgets.
- **Spreadsheet Templates**: Pre-designed templates available in Excel or Google Sheets can help you organize your budget without the need for specialized software.

3. Investment Performance Trackers

Monitoring the performance of your investments ensures that your portfolio aligns with your financial goals and risk tolerance.

- **Investment Platforms**: Brokers like Vanguard, Fidelity, and E*TRADE provide tools to track the performance of your investments.
- **Financial Dashboards**: Platforms like Morningstar and Bloomberg offer comprehensive dashboards that analyze your investment portfolio's performance.

4. Savings Tracking

Keeping track of your savings goals is essential for building an emergency fund and planning for future expenses.

- **Savings Apps**: Tools like Qapital, Acorns, and Digit automate the savings process, helping you set and achieve savings goals.
- **Banking Tools**: Many banks offer built-in tools to track your savings progress and set up automatic transfers to savings accounts.

Adjusting Strategies Based on Results

Once you have collected and analyzed your data, the next step is to adjust your strategies to optimize your networking efforts and financial growth. Here are some approaches to consider:

1. Identify Gaps and Opportunities

- **Analyze Weaknesses**: Determine where your networking efforts are lacking. Are you not attending enough events, or are your interactions too superficial?
- **Spot Opportunities**: Look for areas where you can expand your network or enhance your financial strategies. This could involve targeting new demographics or exploring alternative investment options.

2. Set New Goals

Based on your assessments, set new, achievable goals that address identified gaps and capitalize on opportunities.

- **Networking Goals**: If your number of connections is low, set a target to attend more events or engage more actively on professional platforms.
- **Financial Goals**: If your savings rate is insufficient, adjust your budget to allocate more funds toward savings or explore higher-yield investment options.

3. Reallocate Resources

Effective resource management is key to maximizing your growth potential.

- **Time Management**: Allocate more time to activities that yield higher networking or financial returns. This might mean dedicating specific hours each week to networking events or financial planning.
- **Financial Resources**: Reallocate funds toward investments that offer better returns or prioritize paying down high-interest debt to improve your financial standing.

4. Seek Feedback and Mentorship

Engage with mentors and trusted peers to gain insights and advice on improving your strategies.

- **Feedback Sessions**: Regularly seek feedback on your networking approach and financial strategies to identify areas for refinement.
- **Mentorship**: Leverage the experience of mentors who can provide guidance on navigating challenges and optimizing your growth strategies.

5. Embrace Flexibility

Be prepared to adapt your strategies as circumstances change. Flexibility allows you to respond effectively to new opportunities and unforeseen challenges.

- **Continuous Monitoring**: Regularly review your progress and be willing to pivot your strategies based on what the data indicates.
- **Stay Informed**: Keep abreast of industry trends, economic shifts, and new tools that can enhance your networking and financial strategies.

Practical Examples

Example 1: Networking Adjustment

Situation: Sarah notices that while she has a large number of LinkedIn connections, few of them translate into meaningful professional relationships.

Action: She shifts her strategy to focus on deeper engagements by initiating more one-on-one conversations and setting up informational interviews with key contacts.

Result: Sarah builds stronger relationships, leading to new business opportunities and collaborations that significantly impact her career growth.

Example 2: Financial Strategy Adjustment

Situation: John tracks his net worth and realizes his investments in stocks have underperformed compared to his goals.

Action: He diversifies his portfolio by adding bonds and real estate investments, reducing his exposure to volatile stocks.

Result: John's portfolio becomes more balanced, reducing his overall risk and improving his long-term financial stability.

Conclusion

Measuring your success in both networking and financial growth is essential for continuous improvement and achieving your long-term goals. By utilizing the right tools to assess your progress and being willing to adjust your strategies based on the insights gained, you can ensure that your efforts are aligned with your aspirations. Remember, mastery in networking and net worth is an ongoing journey that requires dedication, adaptability, and a commitment to lifelong learning. As you implement these measurement and adjustment strategies, you position yourself to navigate the complexities of personal and professional growth with confidence and resilience.

o1-mini

You said:

write chapter 25 for the book Mastering Network and Net Worth Chapter 1: Understanding Networking Definition and significance of networking. Different types of networks (personal, professional, social). Chapter 2: The Psychology of Networking Building trust and rapport. Overcoming networking anxiety. Chapter 3: Identifying Your Networking Goals Assessing personal and professional aspirations. Setting measurable networking objectives. Chapter 4: Building Your Personal Brand Crafting your personal story. Importance of online presence (LinkedIn, social media). Part 2: Expanding Your Network Chapter 5: Where to Network Identifying key networking opportunities (conferences, seminars, online platforms). Leveraging community events and local groups. Chapter 6: The Art of Conversation Effective communication skills. Active listening and engagement techniques. Chapter 7: Follow-Up Strategies Importance of timely follow-ups. Best practices for staying connected. Chapter 8: Building a Diverse Network Benefits of diversity in connections. Strategies for reaching out to different demographics. Part 3: Leveraging Your Network for Success Chapter 9: Networking for Opportunities How to identify and seize opportunities through connections. Case studies of successful networking. Chapter 10: Mentorship and Guidance Finding and nurturing mentor-mentee relationships. The role of mentorship in personal growth. Chapter 11: Collaborative Networking Building partnerships for mutual benefit. Examples of successful collaborations. Chapter 12: Networking Etiquette Dos and don'ts of professional networking. Navigating cultural differences in networking.

Part 4: Understanding Net Worth Chapter 13: Defining Net Worth Assets vs. liabilities: what counts? The importance of tracking your net worth. Chapter 14: Financial Literacy Fundamentals Basic financial concepts everyone should know.

Resources for improving financial literacy. Chapter 15: Creating a Budget and Savings Plan Steps to develop a personal budget. Strategies for saving effectively. Chapter 16: Investing Basics Overview of investment options (stocks, bonds, real estate). Risk assessment and portfolio diversification. Part 5: Increasing Your Net Worth Chapter 17: Income Streams Identifying and creating multiple income sources. Passive income strategies. Chapter 18: Leveraging Networking for Financial Gains How to turn connections into clients or business opportunities. Networking tactics for entrepreneurs. Chapter 19: Building a Personal Development Plan Setting goals for career advancement. Investing in skills and education. Chapter 20: Risk Management and Insurance Importance of protecting your assets. Types of insurance to consider. Part 6: Sustaining Success Chapter 21: Giving Back and Community Engagement The role of philanthropy in networking and net worth. Building a legacy through community involvement. Chapter 22: Adapting to Change Staying relevant in a changing economy. Networking in a digital age. Chapter 23: Continuous Learning and Growth Emphasizing lifelong learning. Resources for ongoing education. Chapter 24: Measuring Your Success Tools for assessing networking and financial growth. Adjusting strategies based on results.

ChatGPT

Thought for 4 seconds

Chapter 25: Conclusion

As we reach the culmination of "Mastering Network and Net Worth," it's essential to reflect on the journey you've undertaken and the comprehensive strategies you've acquired to enhance both your networking prowess and financial standing. This final chapter serves as a synthesis of the key concepts discussed throughout the book, reinforcing the interconnectedness of networking and wealth-building while providing actionable insights to sustain and amplify your success moving forward.

Recapping the Journey

Part 1: Understanding Networking

We began by defining networking and highlighting its significance in personal and professional contexts. Understanding the different types of networks—personal, professional, and social—set the foundation for recognizing the diverse avenues through which meaningful connections can be forged.

Part 2: Expanding Your Network

Expanding your network involved identifying strategic opportunities, mastering the art of conversation, and implementing effective follow-up strategies. Building a diverse network not only enriches your interactions but also broadens your access to varied perspectives and opportunities.

Part 3: Leveraging Your Network for Success

In this section, we explored how to transform connections into tangible opportunities. From networking for opportunities and fostering mentorship relationships to collaborative networking and adhering to proper etiquette, each chapter provided actionable strategies to maximize the benefits of your network.

Part 4: Understanding Net Worth

Understanding your net worth was pivotal in assessing your financial health. Differentiating between assets and liabilities and tracking your net worth offered a clear picture of your financial standing, setting the stage for informed financial planning.

Part 5: Increasing Your Net Worth

We delved into various strategies to increase your net worth, including creating multiple income streams, leveraging your network for financial gains, building a personal development plan, and managing risks through appropriate insurance coverage. These chapters emphasized the importance of diversification and proactive financial management.

Part 6: Sustaining Success

Sustaining success involved giving back through philanthropy, adapting to change in a dynamic economy, committing to continuous learning, and measuring your progress. These elements ensured that your growth was not only maintained but also evolved with the changing landscape.

Integrating Networking and Financial Growth

Throughout the book, a recurring theme has been the symbiotic relationship between networking and financial growth. Effective networking amplifies your opportunities, providing access to resources, collaborations, and insights that can accelerate your financial aspirations. Conversely, a solid financial foundation empowers you to invest in relationships, whether through attending events, supporting causes, or offering value to your connections.

Key Takeaways

1. **Strategic Networking**: Approach networking with clear goals, authenticity, and a focus on building meaningful relationships. Quality trumps quantity in your connections.
2. **Continuous Learning**: Embrace lifelong learning to stay relevant and adaptable. Invest in your personal and professional development to enhance your value within your network.
3. **Financial Discipline**: Implement robust financial strategies, including budgeting, saving, investing, and risk management, to build and sustain your net worth.
4. **Adaptability**: Stay agile in the face of change. Whether it's technological advancements, market shifts, or personal circumstances, adaptability ensures sustained growth and resilience.
5. **Giving Back**: Engage in philanthropy and community involvement to enrich your network, build credibility, and leave a lasting legacy.

Actionable Steps Moving Forward

To ensure that the insights and strategies from this book translate into real-world success, consider the following actionable steps:

1. Review and Reflect

Take time to review each chapter's key points. Reflect on how they apply to your current situation and identify areas where you can implement changes or improvements.

2. Set Specific Goals

Based on your reflections, set specific, measurable, achievable, relevant, and time-bound (SMART) goals for both networking and financial growth. Clearly defined goals provide direction and motivation.

3. Create an Action Plan

Develop a detailed action plan outlining the steps you need to take to achieve your goals. Include timelines, resources needed, and milestones to track your progress.

4. Leverage Your Network

Actively apply the networking strategies discussed to expand and strengthen your connections. Seek out mentorship, engage in collaborative projects, and utilize your network for both personal and financial opportunities.

5. Invest in Yourself

Prioritize continuous learning and personal development. Enroll in courses, attend workshops, and seek out resources that enhance your skills and knowledge.

6. Monitor Your Progress

Regularly assess your net worth and networking effectiveness using the tools and metrics outlined in the book. Adjust your strategies based on your findings to stay aligned with your goals.

7. Stay Resilient and Adaptable

Embrace challenges and view them as opportunities for growth. Maintain flexibility in your strategies to navigate the ever-changing economic and professional landscapes.

Embracing the Future

Mastering your network and net worth is an ongoing journey that requires dedication, strategic thinking, and a commitment to personal growth. As you continue to apply the principles and strategies discussed in this book, you will not only achieve financial stability but also cultivate a rich and supportive network that propels you toward greater heights.

Remember, success is not a destination but a continuous process of learning, adapting, and evolving. By integrating effective networking practices with sound financial management, you lay the groundwork for a prosperous and fulfilling future.

Final Thoughts

As you embark on the next chapters of your personal and professional life, keep in mind the interconnectedness of your network and your financial health. Nurture your relationships, invest wisely, and remain committed to your growth. The synergy between these elements will empower you to navigate the complexities of the modern world with confidence and achieve lasting success.

Thank you for joining us on this journey through "Mastering Network and Net Worth." May the strategies and insights provided serve as valuable tools in your quest for personal and financial excellence.

www.ingramcontent.com/pod-product-compliance
Lightning Source LLC
Chambersburg PA
CBHW082246220526
45469CB00009B/2895